WHAT SHOULD I BRING?

Great Gifts for Every Occasion

ALISON BOTELER

BARRON'S

Many thanks…
To Grace Freedson, for making this project possible.
To Jackee Mason, for helping me put this book together.

All inquiries should be addressed to:
Barron's Educational Series, Inc.
250 Wireless Boulevard
Hauppauge, New York 11788

Library of Congress Catalog Card No. 92-3729

International Standard Book No. 0-8120-4941-1

Library of Congress Cataloging-in-Publication Data

Boteler, Alison Molinare.
    What should I bring? : great gifts for every occasion / by Alison Boteler.
        p.   cm.
    Includes index.
    ISBN 0-8120-4941-1
    1. Handcraft.   2. Cookery.   3. Gifts.   I. Title
TT157.B695   1992
745.5—dc20   92-3729
                                                                        CIP

PRINTED IN THE UNITED STATES OF AMERICA
2345   0000   987654321

CONTENTS

◆

INTRODUCTION

What should I bring?…if this question seems to draw a blank, you're not alone. So many events call for giving gifts, and so many of the same ones keep showing up. Not that there's anything wrong with a bouquet of flowers, a box of candy, a bottle of wine…even a clay sheep statue that sprouts grass! After all, "It's the thought that counts." But, with a little extra thought, you can turn common things into uncommon gifts.

If you're tired of searching through shopping malls and mail order catalogues for sources of inspiration, then this book is for you. There's an original gift for every occasion, tailored to suit your schedule. It's not the price of a present that's important. It's the personal touch people appreciate, a little gesture that says "I think you're special." By giving a gift of our time we give a part of ourselves. In the process, we discover an overwhelming sense of satisfaction; we discover the joy of giving.

Time is of the Essence

It seems like most of us borrow time just to finish routine tasks. If the thought of setting up a cottage industry to make preserves or a potpourri seems overwhelming, relax. Handmade gifts really take very little time. Even if you enjoy shopping and have absolutely no craft or culinary skills, there are ways to customize a gift and give it personal meaning. That's what this book is all about. There's something for everyone to give to anyone, for any occasion.

Symbols for Success

Amateur cook or culinary whiz? Novice hobbyist or master craftsman? Short on time or time to spare? There are projects for everyone in this book. Nothing takes special skills or tools. I've keyed the projects so readers can make an appropriate choice. The fastest, easiest ideas have a one-clock symbol.

 1 Clock = *A simple project that can be completed in a short period of time.*

 2 Clocks = *A simple project requiring a longer period of time to prepare.*

 Child's Face = *A project that can be made by a child, or a child-parent assisted effort.*

Sources, Supplies, and Stock to Have on Hand

Almost all the supplies in this book are readily available. Card and stationery stores are a fine source for ribbons and paper. But think beyond the obvious.

Your local florist sells an interesting array of wired ribbons, raffia, and beautiful colored foils. This is also the place to go for floral foam, potting containers, straw, or grapevine wreaths. Many fabric stores carry a full line of craft supplies from fabric paints to feathers. This is the place to go for a hot glue gun, an absolute must-have that has revolutionized modern handicrafts.

When it comes to containers, I stockpile boxes. If I see the perfect size and shape for a particular item, I'll buy several. Card shops, craft stores, and mailing franchises carry a selection of gift boxes.

Other sources worth exploring are craft stores, wholesale restaurant-supply and paper-warehouse outlets that are open to the public. That's where I buy Chinese carry-out cartons, two-piece salad-bar boxes, pie boxes, cake boxes, pizza boxes, plastic trays, cake boards, cellophane bags, labels, tags, and 10-pound rolls of wrapping paper. I'm attracted to the generic quality of everything. Those simple white surfaces are waiting to be decorated. When I use conventional wrapping paper, I only buy large rolls of solid colors, such as red, ivy green, pink, gold, and silver. These are the most versatile year-round colors. Forget those little packages of folded paper; the creases make unsightly gift wrap.

What should you have on hand? That really depends upon your life-style, how often you give gifts, and the kind of gifts you'll make. I once toured a historic Victorian house that had a gift-wrapping room. Obviously the original owners felt obligated to bring a lot of hostess gifts. The concept left a lasting impression on me. I'm certainly not exchanging presents as often as they did, but I still find it convenient to set up a special wrapping station in the house. It makes sense to buy large quantities of some wrapping supplies. There's no waste, as you'll inevitably use these items year after year.

It would be impractical to suggest that you stock all of the materials necessary for the projects in this book. However, the following are craft and packing supplies that will always come in handy:

GLUE GUN (hot melt or low melt)

TACKY-CRAFT GLUE

FABRIC GLUE

PINKING SHEARS

SCISSORS

YARDSTICK / RULER / TAPE MEASURE

ACRYLIC PAINTS IN ASSORTED COLORS

CRAFT BRUSHES

FABRIC-PAINT TUBES (puffy, glitter, and slick)

SPONGES (cellulose and natural)

GOLD AND SILVER SPRAY PAINT

CRAYONS

FELT-TIP MARKERS

BROWN PARCEL PAPER

WHITE FREEZER PAPER

PARCHMENT PAPER

SOLID-COLOR WRAPPING PAPER

TISSUE PAPER IN ASSORTED COLORS

GOLD MYLAR TISSUE AND RAINBOW MYLAR TISSUE

CELLOPHANE AND COLORED PLASTIC WRAPS

CELLOPHANE GRASS IN GOLD, SILVER, AND GREEN

WHITE PAPER LUNCH BAGS

SALAD-BAR BOXES

TWO-PIECE GIFT BOXES

PIE, CAKE, AND PIZZA BOXES

CURLING RIBBON IN ASSORTED COLORS

SATIN AND GROSGRAIN RIBBONS IN ASSORTED COLORS

GOLD ELASTIC GIFT CORD

PLAID RIBBON

3 × 5-INCH UNRULED INDEX CARDS

HOLE PUNCH

STAPLER

NOTARY SEALS WITH MONOGRAMMED EMBOSSER

TRANSPARENT TAPE AND DOUBLE-STICK TAPE

FLORAL WIRE AND TAPE

HOSPITALITY TREATS

Spicy Pecan Purses

Cajun Cocktail Nuts

Goldfish Bowl Bites

Pecan Lace Wafers in "14 Karat Kan"

Pigs' Ears Pastries

Hand-Cut Pecan Peacock Cookies

"Alison's Restaurant" Spinach Salad Pie

"Alison's Restaurant" Peanut-Brittle Bush

Herb Bubble Bread Board

Southwestern-Style Party Pizza

Cabana Banana Pool Party Pizza

◆

Hospitality Treats

Whether you're a dinner guest or a house guest, bringing the host or hostess a token treat is thoughtful. Bottles of wine, bouquets, and baskets are always appropriate. However, this section focuses on taste-tempting goodies to share with your host or hostess. These range in effort from goldfish bowl bites to a peanut brittle bush.

But if you can't cook anything, why not wrap a bottle of champagne in a shirt and tie (See Wine Bottle Wrap-ups). Whatever you do, if you do-it-yourself, you're bound to leave a lasting impression.

Spicy Pecan Purses

MAKES 4 CUPS OR 4 PURSE GIFTS

Buttery pecans laced with sugar and spice are sinfully addictive!

1 cup (2 sticks) unsalted butter

4 cups pecan halves

3 cups powdered sugar

2 Tablespoons cinnamon

1 Tablespoon nutmeg

Preheat oven to 300°F (150°C).

Melt butter in large, heavy skillet; stir in pecans. Saute over low heat for 20 minutes, until nuts are lightly browned. Remove with slotted spoon and drain on food approved paper towels. Sift together sugar and spices; pour into large paper bag. Add pecans and shake until well coated with sugar. Spread pecans out on paper towel-lined cookie sheet. Place in oven. Turn off heat and dry pecans overnight, or 8 hours. Remove from oven.

Provençal Purses

1 yard country French print cotton

Cellophane in coordinating color
(labeled "food-approved")

1 yard 1/2-inch wide satin ribbon
in coordinating color

4 cinnamon sticks (4 to 5 inches)

Cut fabric and cellophane into four, 15-inch squares. Cut ribbon into 9-inch segments. For each bag: Lay cellophane on fabric. Place one cup of pecans in center and gather up ends of fabric and cellophane over pecans. Tie with ribbon. Attach cinnamon stick to each bag using ends of ribbons.

Cajun Cocktail Nuts

MAKES 6 BOWLS OF NUTS; 1 GIFT

These spicy mixed nuts are packaged in wooden salad bowls, just like the ones used for bar "munchies."

$^1\!/_2$ cup (1 stick) butter or margarine, melted

2 Tablespoons Worcestershire sauce

2 teaspoons chili powder

2 to 3 dashes hot pepper sauce

1 pound unsalted peanuts

1 pound raw cashews

2 pounds unsalted, raw pecan halves

Garlic salt

Black pepper

Preheat oven to 275°F (125°C).

Mix butter, Worcestershire, chili powder, and pepper sauce in glass measuring cup. Combine nuts in large roasting pan and drizzle with butter mixture, stirring to coat. Bake 45 minutes, stirring every 15 minutes. Spread out on paper towels (labeled for use with food) to dry. Season with garlic salt and black pepper.

Cellophane-Wrapped Salad Bowls

6 small wooden salad bowls
6 yards red or clear cellophane
6 feet red-checked ribbon
Rubber bands

Divide mixed nuts evenly among bowls. Cut cellophane into
3/4-yard sheets. Cut ribbon into 1-foot lengths. For each bowl:
Center in middle of cellophane sheet. Bring edges up around bowl
and gather cellophane on top. Secure in place with rubber band.
Tie ribbon around rubber band, concealing it. Remove rubber band.
Tie bow with ribbon streamers. Trim top of cellophane tassel with
pinking shears.

Opposite: Candy Mint Cornflowers, page 32

Goldfish Bowl Bites

MAKES 6 CUPS, 3 GIFTS

Party mixes are so popular, they're now everyday snacks. For a new twist, I use goldfish crackers and package them in a real goldfish bowl, topped off with a net.

2 six-ounce bags plain goldfish crackers

1 six-ounce bag cheddar goldfish crackers

1 six-ounce bag pretzel goldfish crackers

1 cup pecan halves

$^1/_2$ cup (1 stick) butter or margarine, melted

1 teaspoon Worcestershire sauce

1 envelope ranch-style salad dressing mix

Preheat oven to 250°F (120°C).

Combine crackers and pecans in large shallow roasting pan. Combine melted butter, Worcestershire, and salad-dressing mix. Pour over crackers; gently stir to coat. Bake 50 minutes, stirring every 15 minutes. Spread out on wax paper to cool.

Opposite: Pig's Ears Pastries, page 11

Goldfish Bowls with Nets

3 one-quart fish bowls with rim at top
¹/₂ yard green net or tulle fabric
Cellophane in clear or blue
³/₄ yard green elastic cord

Fill bowls with cracker mixture. Trace three 8-inch circles with pencil on netting with cellophane under it. Cut circles of cellophane and netting. For each bowl, hold cellophane circle evenly under net circle. Center over the opening of bowl. Cut cord into 3 equal pieces. Tie cord with bow to fit snugly around neck of bowl. Slip elastic over netting, gathering it around the rim.

Pecan Lace Wafers in "14 Karat Kan"

MAKES 3 DOZEN COOKIES; 1 GIFT

These elegant cookies deserve an extravagant container. The top of a can is decorated with pecan halves, then gilded with gold spray paint.

¼ cup (½ stick) butter, softened

½ cup firmly packed light brown sugar

1 egg

¼ cup lightly toasted, finely chopped pecans

2 Tablespoons all-purpose flour

¼ teaspoon salt

Preheat oven to 300°F (150°C).

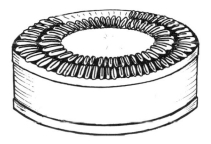

Cream butter and sugar together until blended. Beat in egg, pecans, flour, and salt. Tear off 4 pieces of parchment paper the size of the cookie sheet. Place one piece of paper on cookie sheet and drop nine half-teaspoonfuls of dough 5 inches apart on paper (cookies will spread during baking). Bake for 10 minutes.

Remove from oven and gently slide paper, with cookies on it, onto a counter to cool. Repeat with remaining 3 sheets. When cookies are cool, remove with spatula and store in tightly covered container.

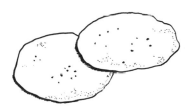

Note: To toast pecans, place on baking sheet in preheated 350°F (175°C) oven for 5 minutes.

14 Karat Kan

9- to 10-inch round cookie can, 4 to 5 inches deep
Metal primer spray
2 cups lightly toasted pecan halves
Extra-strength craft glue
Gold spray paint
Sheet of gold Mylar tissue

Place can lid and bottom facing down on large sheet of aluminum foil. Spray with a coat of metal primer. Dry 24 hours. Glue pecans on lid in a circular pattern beginning at outside edge and working each row of pecans towards the center using extra-strength craft glue. Dry 24 hours. Spray lid and bottom gold, and dry 24 hours. Line inside bottom of can with Mylar tissue, draping about 10 inches of wrap over sides of can. Line with wax paper so cookies do not touch Mylar. Gently layer cookies in can. Bring tissue back up around wax paper and cover with lid.

Pigs' Ears Pastries

MAKES 3 1/2 DOZEN PASTRIES; 1 TIN

Of all cookies, this is perhaps my favorite. I was introduced to palmiers, butterflies, or pigs' ears pastries, to list some of their names, as a small child. We stopped at André's, a Swiss pastry shop in Kansas City, for after-school tea and treats. I still frequent Swiss restaurants. No meal would seem complete without a coupe Toblerone sundae, topped with pigs' ears pastries.

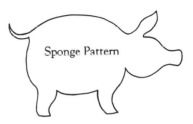

Sponge Pattern

1 sheet frozen puff pastry, defrosted
(about 8 ounces)

Sugar

Preheat oven to 400°F (200°C).

If pastry is too soft and limp, return to refrigerator to chill. Cover pastry board with generous sprinkling of sugar. Spread pastry out on board and coat top with layer of sugar. Roll into a rectangle about 1/4-inch thick. Fold long sides inward, so two edges meet in seam down center. Dust with sugar. Fold edges toward center again. Sprinkle with sugar and fold in half. Wrap in plastic and chill until firm.

Line two cookie sheets with parchment paper. With sharp knife, slice dough about 1/16-inch thick. Place slices 3 inches apart on baking sheet. Sprinkle tops of pastries with pinch of sugar. Bake 8 minutes. Remove from oven and turn cookies over. Bake 7 minutes longer, until crisp and sugar is caramelized. Cool on wire rack and keep stored in airtight container to preserve freshness.

Pig-Print Tin

Drop cloth or aluminum foil
10-inch metal cookie tin 4 to 5 inches deep
Metal primer spray paint
Seafoam-green spray paint
Soft-pink acrylic paint
Metal pie plate
Pig-shaped printing sponge (see Note)
White and black acrylic paint (optional)
20-inch square clear cellophane
(labeled for use with food)
2 yards of ¼-inch pink satin ribbon.

Lay drop cloth over work surface. Open tin and lay lid and base on prepared surface, insides facing down. Spray tin with metal primer. Dry thoroughly. Give tin two coats green paint. Dry thoroughly between each coat. Pour pink paint into metal pie plate. Turn base of tin right-side up. Pat sponge into pink paint and print pigs around sides of can. Print pigs on lid. Dry. If desired, use white paint for pigs' eyes and dot pupils with black paint. Dry thoroughly.

Line box with food approved cellophane and arrange pastries inside. Fold excess cellophane back over pastries and close lid. Tie ribbon around box, crisscrossing underneath and tie in bow on top.

Note: Precut printing sponges are sold in most craft stores. You can make your own by drawing a pattern on a 3/4-inch thick kitchen sponge and cutting it out with scissors. With either commercial or homemade sponge, premoisten and squeeze dry before printing.

Hand-Cut Pecan Peacock Cookies

MAKES 4 DOZEN COOKIES; 4 GIFTS

Use your palm as a pattern for cutting peacocks out of pecan cookie dough. Green candied cherries become the eyes of the tail feathers. (Kids love to lend a helping "hand" with these.)

4 cups all-purpose flour

2 1/2 cups pecans, lightly toasted, finely chopped

1 teaspoon baking powder

1 teaspoon cinnamon

1/2 teaspoon nutmeg

1 cup sugar

1/3 cup sherry or orange juice

1/4 cup light molasses

3/4 cup (1 1/2 sticks) butter or margarine

2 1/2 ounces slivered almonds

6 ounces green candied cherries

6-ounce package semisweet chocolate minichips

Preheat oven to 350°F (175°C).

Combine flour, pecans, baking powder, and spices in large mixing bowl. Heat sugar, sherry, molasses, and butter in saucepan until butter melts. Blend into flour mixture to make soft dough. Chill at least 2 hours.

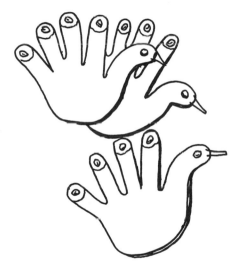

Divide dough into 4 parts. (Keep remaining parts chilled while rolling one out.) Roll dough out 1/4-inch thick on floured surface. Use your hand to trace a pattern in the dough and cut shape with sharp knife. Place dough on cookie sheet lined with parchment paper. The thumb section of cookie is the peacock's head; the fingers are tail feathers.

Insert almond sliver into side edge of head for a beak. Slice cherries very thin, to yield 4-inch "rings." Press rings on top of each tail feather. Place minichip in peacock's head for the eye and in center of each cherry slice, for the "eye" of the tail feather. Use wedge-shaped sliver of green cherry for the "plume" on top of peacock's head.

Bake cookies 10 to 12 minutes, or until lightly browned. When cool, carefully lift from sheet with spatula.

Peacock Boxes

Green cellophane grass
4 large plastic salad-bar boxes
Green, blue, brown, and gold metallic curling ribbon
4 peacock feathers (available from craft shops or florists)

Make nest of grass in bottom of each box. Arrange a dozen cookies in each box. Close lids. Gather a strand of each color ribbon while pulling from rolls and tie all colors around the box, near each corner of box and tying a knot on top. Tie a feather in knot. Trim ribbon edges to about 10 inches and curl with scissors.

"Alison's Restaurant" Spinach Salad Pie

MAKES 8 SERVINGS; 1 GIFT

As a college sophomore, I had a campus radio show called "Alison's Restaurant." It was an interview format featuring guests from the food world. There were some shows I'd rather forget, but others I will remember as milestone moments in my life. Those include my meetings with Craig Claiborne and Julia Child. I always made it a policy to bring a gift to the guest. When I learned I'd be interviewing Craig Claiborne at his home in East Hampton, I was overwhelmed. I was a wide-eyed student in need of a gift good enough for a culinary god. I took my favorite childhood recipe for spinach salad and put it in a pie shell. Craig Claiborne liked it enough to run the recipe in his *New York Times Magazine* column!

2 ten-ounce packages frozen chopped spinach, thawed

3/4 to 1 cup regular or nonfat mayonnaise

2 teaspoons Dijon mustard

1/2 to 1 teaspoon Worcestershire sauce

1/2 cup finely chopped scallions

1/2 cup grated Swiss cheese

Baked 10-inch tart shell
(recipe follows)

1 hard-cooked egg, grated, or 1/4 cup toasted, chopped pecans

Squeeze all moisture from spinach by hand. In a bowl, blend mayonnaise with mustard and Worcestershire. Mix into spinach, with scallions and cheese. Refrigerate several hours. A few hours before serving, spread spinach mixture into cooled tart shell.

15

Sprinkle grated egg inside rim of tart. Carefully remove filled tart from pan.

Preheat oven to 400°F (200°C).

Baked 10-inch Tart Shell: Soften refrigerated sheet of pie pastry or defrosted, frozen pie shell, removed from pan. Ease into 10-inch tart or quiche pan with removable bottom. Press pastry into sides and trim dough to edges of pan. Spray sheet of waxed paper with nonstick cooking spray. Press waxed paper, sprayed-side down, against dough. Fill with raw rice or beans. Bake 8 minutes. Remove paper and rice from pan. Continuing baking 8 to 10 minutes longer. Cool shell completely before filling. This tart is served chilled.

Sponge-Painted Pie Box

*10-inch collapsible white pie box with tabs
(about 2 ¹/₂ to 3 inches high)*

2 shades spinach green acrylic paint

2 metal pie plates

Natural sponge

1 yard green cellophane

10-inch round piece cardboard

1 yard ¹/₂-inch wide green grosgrain ribbon

While box is still flat, pour paints in separate pie plates. Use sponge to make a marble-like print on surface, using one color at a time. Allow paint to dry thoroughly. Assemble box and line bottom with cellophane, allowing excess to drape over sides. Add cardboard round. Place chilled tart on cardboard. Fold cellophane back over top. Close lid and tie ribbon in a bow around box, catching opposite corners.

◆◆◆

"Alison's Restaurant" Peanut-Brittle Bush

MAKES 16 SERVINGS

Part II of the "Alison's Restaurant" list of gifts includes a concoction I gave to Julia Child. When you're only nineteen, what do you bring the culinary queen? A sinfully gooey, candy-like dessert. I borrowed a basic cream puff tower croquembouche and turned it into a chocolate-covered peanut-brittle bush. (Remember, this was back in the "dark ages," before sugar and fat were considered illegal substances.) To this day, I'm amazed that she even ate it. But Julia Child is a very gracious lady. I framed the postcard she sent from her hotel, thanking me for the great invention.

If you have chocoholic friends with uninhibited eating habits, this will really hit the spot. It makes a dramatic table centerpiece and can be broken off in small pieces. That way, no one feels too guilty.

²/₃ cup butter or margarine

1 ¼ cups water

1 ¼ cups all-purpose flour

¼ cup cocoa

4 teaspoons sugar

5 eggs

Peanut-Brittle Filling
(recipe follows)

Chocolate Glaze
(recipe follows)

8-inch plate or cake base

²/₃ cup chopped peanut brittle

Preheat oven to 400°F (200°C).

Bring butter and water to rolling boil in large saucepan. Stir in flour, cocoa, and sugar, all at once. Lower heat and stir vigorously until mixture forms ball. Remove from heat and beat in eggs, one at a time, to form smooth dough.

Drop by slightly rounded teaspoonfuls onto ungreased cookie sheet. Bake until puffed and crisp. Cool completely.

Fill a large pastry bag with peanut-brittle filling. Make a slit in each puff. Pipe filling into puffs, through opening. Dip bottom of each puff in glaze and cover 8-inch plate with puffs. Sprinkle lightly with crushed peanut brittle. Add another layer of chocolate-dipped puffs. Continue stacking puffs and brittle using fewer puffs for each layer.

The result is a mountain 6 or 7 layers high, with one puff on top. Drizzle any remaining glaze over puffs and sprinkle with peanut brittle. Keep refrigerated until serving time.

Peanut-Brittle Filling

1 pint heavy cream
3 Tablespoons firmly packed dark brown sugar
1 teaspoon vanilla extract
¹⁄₃ cup crushed peanut brittle

Combine all ingredients in bowl of electric mixer and beat at medium speed until stiff peaks form.

Chocolate Glaze

1/2 cup (1 stick) butter or margarine

3 ounces unsweetened chocolate

3 cups powdered sugar

2 teaspoons vanilla extract

3 to 6 Tablespoons hot water

Melt butter and chocolate in saucepan over low heat. Remove from heat. Blend in sugar, vanilla, and enough water to make smooth glaze. It may be necessary to add additional hot water while working with glaze.

Rainbow Volcano Wrap

4 yards clear or colored cellophane
labeled for use with food

Rubber band

2 yards each of 5 assorted colors curling ribbon

Cut cellophane into two 2-yard sheets. Place sheets crisscrossed on large table, and set peanut-brittle bush in center. Bring sides of cellophane up around bush, gathering into tassel at top. Secure with rubber band. Cut ribbons into 1-yard lengths. Hold all 10 streamers together and tie in a tight knot, just under rubber band. Remove rubber band. Curl streamers with scissors and trim tip of tassel with pinking shears.

◆◆◆

Herb Bubble Bread Board

MAKES 4 SERVINGS; 1 GIFT

No "knead" to fear bread baking. This buttery loaf is made by breaking frozen dough into little bubbles. Packaged with a crock of Boursin cheese and a cutting board, it's a guaranteed compliment-getting gift.

1-pound loaf white or honey wheat
frozen bread dough, thawed
$1/3$ cup melted butter
$1/2$ teaspoon garlic powder
$1/2$ teaspoon thyme
$1/2$ teaspoon crushed rosemary
$1/2$ teaspoon celery seeds
$1/4$ teaspoon sage
1 teaspoon dill
$1/3$ to $1/2$ cup grated Parmesan cheese

Preheat oven to 375°F (190°C).

Use scissors to cut loaf into 20 pieces. Combine melted butter with seasonings in small bowl. Place cheese in shallow dish. Shape dough pieces into balls. Dip in butter mixture and roll in cheese. Arrange balls in greased 8 × 4-inch loaf pan. Cover with clean, dry towel and let rise in warm place until doubled in bulk. Bake until golden brown. Cool 10 minutes and invert from pan.

Herb Bread Board

1/2 yard 1/2-inch wide ivy green grosgrain ribbon
2 yards 30-inch wide clear cellophane (food approved)
Wooden bread board
12-inch square ivy-green gingham with pinked edges
4 ounce container Boursin or other herb cheese
Serrated knife with wooden handle

Cut ribbon in half and cellophane into one 3/4-yard and one 1 1/4-yard lengths. Tie 3/4-yard length cellophane around cooled bread, gathering at one end. Tie with ribbon. Trim cellophane tassel with pinking shears.

Line bread board with gingham, arranging square diagonally. Place wrapped bread on board, along with cheese and knife. Wrap board in 1 1/4-yard length cellophane. Gather edges around knife handle. Secure in place by tying remaining ribbon around handle. Trim edges of cellophane with pinking shears.

Southwestern-Style Party Pizza

MAKES 8 TO 10 SERVINGS; 2 PIZZA GIFTS

This Southwestern version of pizza is surprisingly simple and more personalized than the average pizza.

12-ounce bottle chili sauce

8-ounce bottle salsa

1 Tablespoon chili powder

1/2 cup chopped green bell pepper

16-ounce jar baby corn cobs, drained

10-ounce package brown and serve beef sausages

Southwestern Pizza Dough
(recipe follows)

16-ounce package shredded Monterey Jack cheese

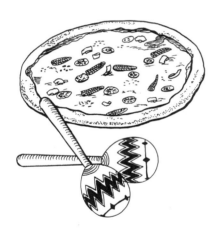

Preheat oven to 400°F (200°C).

In bowl, combine chili sauce, salsa, chili powder, and green pepper. Split baby corn cobs in half lengthwise. Slice sausages into 1/2-inch rounds. Saute in skillet until browned about 5 minutes. Drain on paper towels. Spread chili sauce mixture on pizza dough. Top with corn cobs and sausage. Sprinkle with grated cheese. Bake pizzas 15 minutes.

Opposite: Crudite Bouquet, page 33

Southwestern Pizza Dough

1 package active dry yeast

2 Tablespoons warm water (105° to 115°)

1 teaspoon salt

2 Tablespoons olive oil

1 Tablespoon honey

1 egg, well beaten

2 cups all-purpose flour

1 cup cornmeal

1 cup cold water

Dissolve yeast in warm water; blend in salt, oil, honey, and egg. Combine flour and cornmeal in large bowl, blend in yeast mixture and cold water. Do not let dough rise. Knead on lightly floured surface for 3 minutes. Divide into two balls. Roll out each ball and line 13-inch pizza pan that has been lightly greased and sprinkled with cornmeal.

Opposite: Antipasto Plant, page 36

Bandana Boxes

1 yard, 45-inch red bandana-print cotton
2 thirteen-inch pizza boxes
Moveable spray-mount adhesive
Tacky craft glue
X-Acto knife
3 yards red grosgrain ribbon, cut in half

Cut fabric into two 18 × 45-inch sections.

Open each box flat. Spray wrong side of fabric with adhesive. Place outside of box against fabric. Turn over and smooth out any lumps or wrinkles. Turn over and cut around curved tab corners to edge of cardboard, but allow 1/2-inch selvage along straight edges. Apply thin film of tacky craft glue along selvages and fold over onto cardboard. Using X-Acto knife cut through tab slots. (Method described in "Covered Boxes" of Box Basics.) Fold box along original creases and put together. Place pizzas in box and cover with lid. Take a 1 1/2-yard length of ribbon and tie around each box, catching corners diagonally. Tie ribbon in bow at one corner.

Note: Pizza can be brought unbaked to a party, then baked just before serving. And, to save time you can substitute ready-made refrigerated pizza dough for this Southwestern-style dough, although the cornmeal texture will be lacking.

Cabana Banana Pool Party Pizza

MAKES 8 TO 10 SERVINGS; 1 PIZZA GIFT

For a pool party with a tropical touch, try this pie disguised as a pizza. Coconut crunch tops a filling of pineapple and bananas for a Caribbean flavor.

*2 nine-inch frozen pie shells, defrosted
or 2 refrigerated pastry crusts*

*1 sixteen-ounce can and 1 eight-ounce can
pineapple chunks, drained*

3 medium bananas, peeled and sliced

2/3 cup sugar

2 teaspoons cornstarch

1 teaspoon cinnamon

1/4 teaspoon nutmeg

Coconut Crunch Topping
(recipe follows)

Preheat oven to 450°F (230°C).

If using frozen pie shells, remove from pans. If using refrigerated pie crusts, remove wrapping. Stack pie crusts together. Roll out on floured surface to 15-inch circle. Ease into 13-inch pizza pan. Trim pastry and crimp for smooth-edged rim resembling a pizza. Distribute pineapple chunks and banana slices evenly on pastry. Combine sugar, cornstarch, and spices in small bowl. Sprinkle over fruit. Cover with topping. Bake 30 to 35 minutes, until pastry edges are golden brown.

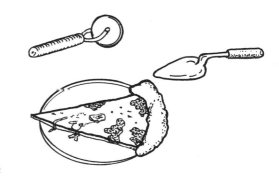

Coconut Crunch Topping

3/4 cup all-purpose flour
1/3 cup shredded coconut
1/2 cup firmly packed light brown sugar
1/2 cut (1 stick) butter or margarine, chilled

Combine flour, coconut, and sugar in mixing bowl. With pastry blender, cut in butter until mixture is crumbly.

Cabana Striped Boxes

Cover one pizza box as described in Southwestern party pizza and the section on "Covered Boxes" in Box Basics. Use a striped, glazed chintz fabric or wallpaper. Pink and white, yellow and white, or green and white stripes are all very effective in creating a Caribbean atmosphere. Tie box with ribbon matching the stripes.

2

BOUQUETS AND BASKETS

Sand Pail of Snapdragons and Soap

Candy Mint Cornflowers

Crudite Bouquet

Antipasto Plant

Ribbon-Laced Strawberry Basket

Vanilla Wafer Mushrooms

Mushroom Meringue Cookie Crate

Brunch Bread Basket of Banana Muffins

Pecan Pinecone Cookies in a Pinecone Basket

Pesto Pasta Dinner Basket

Fanciful Dried Flowers

Potpourri Pointers

Quick-Fix Baskets

◆

Bouquets and Baskets

◆◆

If you think of bouquets in terms of something you order from the florist, think again. Arrangements come from an array of sources. Be it garden flowers, dried-herb nosegays, candy cornflowers, or antipasto plants, bouquets brighten any day. You can create stunning gifts by simply using some supermarket flowers.

Baskets are another popular item. Several of the basket projects in this section take a minimum of effort, especially when you use suggested shortcuts. For a splendid gift, you simply can't miss with a beautiful basket.

Sand Pail of Snapdragons and Soap

MAKES 1 GIFT

Seashell or snail bath soaps are a bonus gift, blossoming from a beautiful bouquet of snapdragons. When presented in a child's sand pail, this makes a whimsical summer arrangement.

Cube of oasis or floral foam
Child's sand pail, about 8 inches high
12 to 15 fresh snapdragons
Baby's breath or other filler foliage
Nail or ice pick
12 small seashell or snail bath soaps
12 nine-inch floral picks

Push oasis into sand pail, trimming to fit snugly. Moisten with water. Arrange snapdragons by trimming to varying lengths, cutting stems at an angle. Insert into oasis. Fill in with baby's breath. Using nail, pierce hole in bottom of each soap. Push floral picks into holes. Arrange soaps throughout bouquet, inserting floral picks into oasis.

Tulle Wrap

72-inch square of tulle in shade to complement flowers
Rubber band
1 yard 1/2-inch wide satin ribbon to match

Place sand pail in center of tulle on large work surface. Bring edges of tulle up around bouquet and gather in a tassel at top being careful to not crush or crown flowers. Secure tassel with rubber band. Cut ribbon into one 12-inch and one 24-inch piece. Tie 24-inch piece around rim of pail in bow. Tie 12-inch piece just underneath rubber band in bow. Remove rubber band. Trim edges of tulle with pinking shears.

Candy Mint Cornflowers

MAKES 1 BOUQUET

A delightful bouquet of refreshing blue mints and lemon sour balls, blossoming from a pot of fresh mint leaves.

12 nine-inch green floral picks

12 lemon sour balls wrapped in cellophane

Green floral tape

4 dozen ice blue mint hard candies,
wrapped in cellophane

Holding pick in one hand, tape one sour ball at end using green floral tape (Fig. 1). Hold 4 mint candies by wrapper tails and arrange around yellow candy on stick. Start winding tape around wrappers and down stick to attach (Fig. 2). Repeat with remaining picks and candies.

Fig.1   Fig.2

Fresh Mint Flowerpot

1 twenty-inch square of yellow cellophane

2 twenty-inch squares of yellow tissue paper

2 twenty-inch squares of blue tissue paper

1 mint plant (medium size) in a 5 inch pot

1 yard each blue and yellow 1/4-inch wide satin ribbon

Make a stack of wrappings with yellow cellophane on top, then yellow tissue, then blue tissue. Place plant in center of cellophane. Bring tissue edges up around pot. Tie both ribbons around rim of pot in a bow. Arrange candy flowers in soil around plant (Fig. 3).

Fig.3

◆◆◆

Crudité Bouquet

MAKES 12 APPETIZER SERVINGS; 1 GIFT

Rosy radishes and exotic endive lilies blossom from a broccoli bush. Asparagus add an interesting dimension to the arrangement. A carved-out cabbage acts as a floral oasis and a vessel for a cheesy chive dip.

12 small heads Belgian endive

2 dozen radishes

12 to 18 asparagus spears

2 to 4 dozen broccoli florets

Cheesy Chive Dip
(recipe follows)

Fig.1

Gently separate heads of endive, pulling leaves apart, but not off (Fig. 1). Cut thin slashes across radishes (Fig. 2). Soak overnight in ice water so leaves and slices spread. Bring 3 quarts water to boil. Drop in a few pieces of asparagus and broccoli. After 30 seconds remove vegetables with slotted spoon. Immediately immerse vegetables in ice-cold water to stop cooking. Repeat with remaining broccoli and asparagus. Drain vegetables and chill overnight. Meanwhile, prepare cheesy chive dip and chill overnight.

Fig.2

Cheesy Chive Dip

1 cup milk

3 ounces grated cheddar cheese

2 tablespoons grated Parmesan cheese

1 envelope ranch-style dressing mix (regular milk recipe)

1 cup mayonnaise (regular or nonfat)

1 tablespoon fresh minced chives

Combine milk, cheeses, and salad dressing in blender. Blend until cheddar cheese is pureed. Combine mayonnaise and chives in bowl. Pour milk mixture over mayonnaise, blending with wire whisk. Pour into jar or cheese crock and chill.

Broccoli Bush

1 large cabbage

3 dozen chives or scallion stems

Radish roses

Endive lilies

Blanched broccoli and asparagus

3 dozen 9-inch wooden skewers

1 large, shallow glass or silver bowl
slightly larger than base of the cabbage

Wooden toothpicks

Gold or green floral foil

Hollow out inside of cabbage, leaving 1 1/2-inch wall. Insert skewers
through the base of chives and up through shaft to resemble stems.
Insert stems into bases of radishes and endive (Fig. 3). Insert
toothpicks into the base of broccoli florets and stick florets all over
cabbage. Use toothpicks in base of asparagus to insert in spaces
between broccoli. Insert "flowers" in an artistic balance. Put bush
in bowl. Wrap arrangement in a large tent of floral foil, and carry
dip separately.

Fig.3

◆◆◆

Antipasto Plant

MAKES 6 TO 8 APPETIZER SERVINGS; 1 GIFT

As with the crudite bouquet, an antipasto bush combines familiar foods into a faux floral arrangement. To avoid wilting, this whimsical gift should be assembled only a few hours before presentation.

3 dozen 8- or 9-inch wooden skewers

Chives or green stems of scallions

6 marinated artichoke hearts, well drained

3 cherry tomatoes, halved

6 pimiento-stuffed olives

6 slices salami

6 ears baby corn cobs

6 slices smoked turkey

6 cornichons or gherkins

6 strips proscuitto

6 wedges pickled watermelon

6 pumpernickel snack sticks

Fig.1   Fig.2

Fig.3   Fig.4   Fig.5

Makes stems for appetizers by inserting skewers through cut end of chives. Attach base of artichokes on end of 6 stems. Scoop out inside pulp of cherry tomato halves. Stick tomatoes on 6 stems with olive in center of each tomato (Fig. 1). Fold salami in half, then roll up in a cone around piece of baby corn. Anchor onto 6 stems, sticking through salami and corn (Fig. 2). Fold and roll turkey around cornichons and attach to 6 stems the same way (Fig. 3).

Wrap proscuitto around watermelon and stick on 6 stems (Fig. 4). Carefully insert 6 stems into bottoms of pumpernickel snack sticks to resemble cat tails (Fig. 5). Be careful or they'll crack.

Note: All appetizers may be prepared ahead of time. Place on tray, cover with plastic wrap, and refrigerate overnight.

Pumpernickel Planter

*Firm round loaf of pumpernickel bread,
about 1 pound*

*2 heads curly endive, washed
and crisped in refrigerator*

2 yards green cellophane

Rubber band

*1/2-yard each: green, white,
and orange curling ribbon*

Hollow cavity in top of bread, leaving thick base and walls around sides. Separate endive leaves and stick ends into loaf, so tips fall over sides of bread like foliage in a flowerpot. Insert stems of appetizers into foliage, anchoring in base of bread. Place finished planter in center of cellophane sheet. Bring cellophane up around sides of arrangement and gather in tassel at top. Secure in place with rubber band. Hold ribbons together and tie around cellophane, just underneath rubber band. Remove rubber band. Curl ribbon streamers and trim top of cellophane.

Antipasto Plant

Ribbon-Laced Strawberry Basket

MAKES 1 QUART BASKET OR 2 PINT BASKET GIFTS

I can't think of anyone who doesn't go into ecstasy over this simple gift. It really is easy to make, and so elegant.

1 quart or 2 pints strawberries in green plastic basket, with grid siding

1 2-ounce package semisweet chocolate chips

1 Tablespoon butter-flavored shortening

1/2 cup shelled, chopped unsalted pistachio nuts

Wash strawberries and thoroughly pat dry. Set on paper-towel lined tray while preparing chocolate. Melt chocolate and shortening in top of a double boiler over simmering water. Stir chocolate until smooth.

Fig.1

Grasp each strawberry by stem end. Dip strawberry 3/4 of the way into melted chocolate, allowing excess to drip off. Place coated berries on foil-lined tray and immediately sprinkle lightly with pistachios. (Use one hand to dip berries; the other to sprinkle nuts.) When all strawberries are dipped, refrigerate tray until chocolate sets, about 20 minutes.

Ribbon-Laced Baskets
(instructions for quart basket)

1 1/2 yards each of 5/8-inch wide satin ribbon
in 3 different pastel colors
Reserved quart basket from strawberries
Clear cellophane

Cut a 1/2-yard piece from each ribbon and reserve for tying
cellophane. Take 1 yard of ribbon and weave in and out of one row
of basket slats, starting and ending at same corner. Repeat with
2 more ribbons and 2 more rows. Tie each row with a bow (Fig. 1).
Carefully remove strawberries from foil, and gently pile into basket.
Braid 3 remaining 1/2-yard lengths of ribbon and knot each end.
Cut braid in half, and knot cut ends. Cut about one yard of cellophane and wrap tube-style around basket. Keep basket centered
and tape seam under basket. Seal each end piece of ribbon braid.
Trim ends of cellophane with pinking shears and spread out.
Keep strawberries refrigerated.

Note: These will only last about two days.

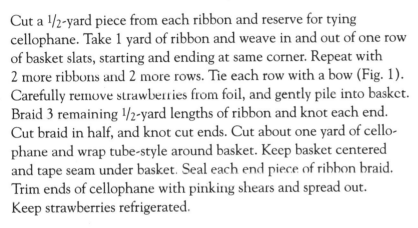

Opposite: *Mushroom Meringue Cookie Crate, page 41*

Vanilla Wafer Mushrooms

MAKES 40 COOKIES, 1–4 GIFTS

For an almost instant yule-time treat, "mushrooms" made of store bought wafers go into a delicious present that is easy to make. The wafers form the mushroom caps and the marshmallows are the "stems." What glues them together is melted chocolate. This and the following recipe can be packaged in the mushroom crates.

1 package vanilla wafer cookies

1-pound package of marshmallows

12-ounce package semisweet chocolate chips

1 Tablespoon butter-flavored vegetable shortening

Marshmallow

Chocolate

Vanilla Wafer

Melt chocolate with shortening in top of double boiler over simmering water. Stir until smooth. Spread chocolate on bottoms of wafers and gently push marshmallow stems into the chocolate. When mushrooms are finished, immediately pack in an airtight container until ready for packaging.

Brunch Bread Basket of Banana Muffins

MAKES 12 MUFFINS; 1 GIFT

Whether you're an overnight guest, or you're hosting an overnight guest, a brunch bread basket is bound to be a hit the next morning. Refrigerated breadsticks make this impressive basket presentation a cinch to bake.

2 eleven-ounce cans refrigerated soft bread sticks

1 egg beaten with 1 Tablespoon water

Toothpicks

Double Banana Muffins
(recipe follows)

Preheat oven to 350°F (175°C).

Invert two 1 1/2-quart ovenproof bowls on a cookie sheet. Cover both bowls with foil, molding to sides. (Don't use heavy duty foil.) Unroll dough and separate into 16 strips. Wrap 13 strips of dough around one foil-covered bowl, twisting as you wrap. Braid remaining 3 strips of dough and place over second bowl to form handle. Bake 20 minutes. Cool 5 minutes.

Brush basket and handle with beaten egg. Loosely cover handle with foil. Bake both an additional 7 to 10 minutes, or until deep golden brown. Cool completely. Remove bread from bowls and peel away foil. Attach handle to sides of bowl with toothpicks. Fill with muffins.

Banana Muffins

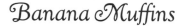

1 egg, well beaten

1 cup milk

1/4 cup (1/2 stick) butter, melted
and cooled to room temperature

1/3 cup firmly packed dark brown sugar

1 Tablespoon baking powder

2 cups all-purpose flour

1/2 cup toasted chopped pecans

1/2 teaspoon banana flavoring (optional)

1/4 teaspoon nutmeg

1 medium banana, mashed

1/2 cup crushed, dried banana chips

Preheat oven to 400°F (200°C).

Combine egg, milk, butter, sugar, baking powder, flour, pecans, flavoring, nutmeg, and banana in bowl. Stir with fork just until blended. Grease bottoms only of muffin tins. Spoon in batter filling 3/4 full. Sprinkle tops with crushed banana chips. Bake 20 to 25 minutes. Cool 10 minutes. Remove from pans.

Brunch Bread Basket Wrap

12-inch square yellow gingham fabric
with pinked edges

3 yards yellow cellophane

Rubber band

1/2 yard 1/2-inch wide yellow satin ribbon

Line inside of basket with gingham. Arrange muffins in basket.
Cut cellophane into two 1 1/2-yard sheets. Crisscross sheets on table.
Place basket in center of cellophane. Bring edges up around sides,
gathering in tassel at top. Secure with rubber band. Tie ribbon in
bow just underneath rubber band. Remove rubber band. Trim top
of tassel with pinking shears.

Pecan Pinecone Cookies

Pecan Pinecone Cookies in a Pinecone Basket

MAKES 24 COOKIES; 1 GIFT

This is an exquisite gift that requires patience rather than skill. Buttery, brown-sugar shortbread is studded with pecans to resemble pinecones.

½ cup (1 stick) unsalted butter or margarine, softened

½ cup firmly packed dark brown sugar

2 teaspoons vanilla extract

1 ½ cups all-purpose flour

About 1 ½ cups pecans

Preheat oven to 350°F (175°C).

Cream butter, sugar, and vanilla together. Blend in flour to make smooth dough. Shape dough into 2 dozen balls. Press balls with fingers, making elongated pinecone shapes. Place at least 2 inches apart on cookie sheet lined with parchment paper.

Insert one pecan into narrowest end of each cookie. Overlap with a second row of 2 pecans. Use 3 pecans on the third row to create pinecone-like nut cluster. Bake 12 to 15 minutes, or until cookies are set. Cool completely on cookie sheet before removing.

Pinecone Basket

Hot glue gun

*Small to medium-sized basket without handle,
dark-wood stained*

Craft-quality pinecones (available in craft stores)

1 to 2 cups of metallic gold cellophane grass

Use hot glue gun to cover basket with pinecones. Line basket with
grass and arrange cookies in basket.

Pesto Pasta Dinner Basket

MAKES 4 SERVINGS; 1 GIFT

This colander, used as a basket, is brimming with the makings of a pasta dinner. Long after the tortellini has been consumed, the colander will continue to provide pasta pleasures.

Pasta Dinner Basket

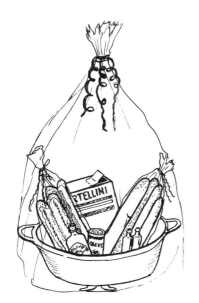

1 head romaine lettuce

Roll clear cellophane

Red, white, and orange curling ribbon

Pesto sauce
(purchased or made with recipe below)

Walnut bread sticks
(purchased or made with recipe below)

Small bottle of extra virgin olive oil

Small bottle balsamic vinegar

Small shaker grated Parmesan cheese

Package sun-dried tomatoes

1 pound vacuum-pack package tri-colored tortellini

Large colander or strainer

Rubber band

No need to wash lettuce. Cut off 1 yard cellophane and roll up lettuce in it. Cut 12-inch lengths of each color ribbon and tie both ends of roll. Repeat with bread sticks, wrapping in roll. Curl ribbon streamers with scissors.

Arrange lettuce, olive oil, vinegar, cheese, tomatoes, tortellini, pesto sauce, and bread sticks in colander. Cut long sheets of cellophane and place crisscross on large work surface. Bring sides of cellophane up around colander and gather at top. Secure tassel with rubber band. Trim tassel to about 5 inches with pinking shears. Cut 24-inch lengths of all three ribbons. Hold together and tie around tassel, just underneath rubber band. Remove rubber band. Curl streamers with scissors.

Pesto Sauce

*2 packed cups fresh basil leaves,
washed and thoroughly dried*

1 to 2 cloves crushed garlic

1/2 cup toasted pine nuts or slivered almonds

1 cup extra-virgin olive oil

3/4 cup grated Parmesan cheese

1/4 cup heavy cream

Salt and cracked black pepper to taste

Combine basil, garlic, and pine nuts in bowl of food processor or blender. Add olive oil in slow, steady stream while running processor. Turn processor off. Add cheese and cream. Process until smooth. Season with salt and pepper. Pour into attractive 12-ounce jar. Refrigerate.

Walnut Bread Sticks

$^{1}\!/_{2}$ cup chopped walnuts
$^{1}\!/_{4}$ cup grated Parmesan cheese
1 can refrigerated bread sticks (8 count)

Combine nuts and cheese in shallow dish. Separate bread sticks and stretch each to 9- to 10-inch length. Roll bread sticks in nut mixture to coat. Bake according to package directions.

Fanciful Dried Flowers

Our ancestors captured a hint of summer during the dreary winter by drying flowers and preserving them. In colonial times, keeping rooms (cool, dry spaces) were decked with bunches of hanging hydrangeas, delphiniums, baby's breath, and even roses.

Dried flowers are an invaluable source for year-round flower arrangements and decorative gift accents. They survive in dark offices where fresh plants often fail.

There's really no mystique about drying flowers. Simply tie the ends of stems together in small bunches and hang upside down for 4 to 7 weeks. This is a delightful doorway treatment between a dining room and kitchen area. Almost any flower can be dried in this way. However, if you're in a hurry, you can use a commercial desiccant (drying agent) like silica gel. Glycerine is useful for drying leafy greens.

Silica Gel: Cover bottom of a cookie tin with silica crystals. Place flowers in tin and spoon crystals onto petals. Cover with lid and seal with tape. Dried flowers will be ready in 48 hours.

Glycerine: Use ferns or leafy greens, such as eucalyptus. Cut the base of stems at an angle. Make a mixture of 40 percent glycerine and 60 percent almost boiling water. Fill vases halfway with mixture and place stems in glycerine water. Allow to dry in a cool dark room for about 6 to 10 days, depending upon humidity.

Note: Flower blossoms may also be pressed between sheets of waxed paper in heavy books. Drying time is similar to that of air-dried flowers.

Dried Roses
(Hanging from Hook)

Potpourri Pointers

Potpourri is popping up everywhere, in every imaginable aroma. Apple potpourri can be simmered on top of the stove, spreading the smell of freshly baked apple pie around the house. For all practical purposes, any potpourri projects in this book can easily be made from store-bought blends. In fact, I find dozens of fragrances right in my own supermarket.

For the purist, making potpourri is a special gift in its own right. It's a mix of dried flower petals, leaves, herbs, and spices. The aroma comes from the addition of concentrated oils. The dried mix soaks up the scent and becomes the ideal vehicle for the fragrance. The following recipes are for the two most popular potpourri: rose and lavender.

Rose Potpourri

2 cups dried rose petals

2 dozen crushed eucalyptus leaves

3 dried rosemary stems, crushed

13 dried sage leaves, crushed

1 teaspoon orrisroot powder
(available in supermarket floral
departments or nurseries)

4 to 5 drops concentrated rose oil

Combine ingredients and store in covered container until ready to use.

Lavender Potpourri

2 cups dried lavender leaves

1 cup dried lavender flower buds

3 dried rosemary stems, crushed

$1/2$ cup dried cornflowers

$1/2$ cup bayberries or juniper berries

1 teaspoon orrisroot powder

3 to 4 drops lavender oil

Combine ingredients and store in a covered container until ready to use.

Bermuda Bath Basket

Quick-Fix Baskets

These gift baskets can be put together in next to no time.

Bermuda Bath Basket: Fill bath or shower caddy with seashell soaps and natural sea sponge. Include premium-quality shampoo, bath gelee, moisturizer, body powder, and after-bath cologne. Add a few real sea shells and wrap in a fishnet.

Banana-Split Basket: Fill an elongated basket with glass or ceramic banana-split dishes. Add an ice cream scoop, jars of sundae toppings, maraschino cherries, chopped nuts, a bunch of bananas. Wrap basket with cellophane and ribbon, enclosing a card with a coupon to the local ice cream or yogurt parlor.

Cajun-Cooking Kit: This is actually a skillet, not a basket. Fill a cast-iron frying pan with jars of Cajun spices, bags of red beans, tasso ham or andouille sausage, pecans, and a cookbook by Paul Prudhomme or Justin Wilson.

Barbecue Bucket: Prepare apple orchard barbecue sauce (see House Dressings and Condiments) or purchase your own favorite brand. Fill a paint bucket with sauce, tongs, basting brush and spare-rib bibs.

◆◆◆

Banana Split Basket

Cajun Cooking Kit

Opposite: Brunch Bread Basket of Banana Muffins, page 43

3

HOUSE DRESSINGS AND CUSTOM CONDIMENTS

Basic Water-Bath Processing
Creamy Champagne Dressing
Six-Pack of Poppy-Seed Dressing
Vermont-Style Maple Bacon Salad Dressing
Homemade Fruit and Herb Vinegars
Safari Sauce
Apple Orchard Barbecue Sauce
Watermelon Rind Relish
Swiss Chocolate Sundae Sauce

Opposite: *Creamy Champagne Dressing, page 59*
Vermont-Style Maple Bacon Salad Dressing, page 63

House Dressings and Custom Condiments

How often have you patronized a favorite restaurant, wishing you could bring home a bottle of the signature salad dressing? Chances are that it's either top secret or for sale in the lobby. Perhaps you can't visit a country inn without loading up on its own label of relishes and preserves. Well, why not whip up a batch of something special with *your* own label?

The nature of the product determines the type of container and how it should be handled. Unless a salad dressing is based only on oil and vinegar, it must be refrigerated at all times. Proteins such as eggs, dairy products, and meat will spoil. However, the bonus of a homemade dressing is that there's no unpleasant preservative aftertaste. Most preserves, jellies, and relishes can be heat-sealed to stand at room temperature. Once opened, they must be refrigerated. Water-bath processing is a technique that boils the contents for a second time, while in sealed jars. This method requires that jars and lids be sterilized in boiling water, and used while hot. If it sounds complicated, don't worry, it's not. In fact, many people find sauce and condiment gifts much simpler to make than baking projects. Besides, there are so many creative ways to embellish bottles and jars.

Basic Water-Bath Processing

You should always have a large kettle of water for both sterilizing and water-bath processing. The same kettle is used for both steps.

To Sterilize Jars: Using tongs, place open jars and separate lids in boiling water. It helps to set jars on their sides, so the cavities fill with water. Boil for at least 5 minutes to ensure sterilization. Remove jars with tongs and place upside-down on clean paper towels to drain. Place lids on paper towels. Fill jars while hot.

Water-Bath Processing: Fill jar with contents to within 1/2 inch of top. Seal with warm lids. Use tongs to stand jars upright in kettle of water. If necessary, adjust the water level so that it comes to within 1/2 inch of jar tops. Bring water to a rolling boil and process for the required period of time called for in the recipe. This usually ranges from 5 to 15 minutes.

Note: Condiments that are preserved using this process must be kept refrigerated at all times after the vacuum seal has been opened.

Creamy Champagne Dressing

MAKES 2 BOTTLES; 2 GIFTS

Easy, yet elegant, Champagne dressing makes a dramatic impact when poured into real Champagne bottles. Substitute reduced-fat versions for the mayonnaise and sour cream in the recipe and this dressing becomes a dieter's dream.

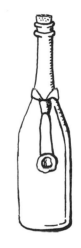

$^1/_2$ cup fresh, minced chives
(or $^1/_4$ cup dried)

3 shallots, finely chopped

1 Tablespoon mustard seed

2 teaspoons cracked black pepper

$^1/_2$ teaspoon celery seed

3 cups flat Champagne

1 pint mayonnaise

1 pint sour cream

1 to 2 teaspoons salt

Combine chives, shallots, mustard seed, pepper, celery seed, and Champagne in saucepan. Bring to a boil. Reduce heat to low and cook liquid down to 2 cups. Refrigerate 2 hours.

With wire whisk, gradually blend liquid into mayonnaise in bowl. Blend in sour cream. Stir in salt to taste.

Note: Reduced-fat mayonnaise contains stabilizers and some brands will produce a slightly thicker dressing.

Hand-Stamped Champagne Bottles

2 Champagne bottles (750 ml) with corks
2 feet of ¹/₂-inch wide gold ribbon
Gold sealing wax with candle wick
Sealing wax stamp (with an initial or other emblem)

Soak labels off bottles. Wash bottles and dry thoroughly. Cut ribbon in half. Tie ribbon around each bottle with necktie-type knot. On each bottle, paste down ends of ribbon by covering with a puddle of hot wax. Stamp initial or emblem in center of wax, while warm. Cover bottles with plastic wrap or paper towels to protect from drips. Pour dressing into bottles. Seal with corks and refrigerate. (Corks may need to be trimmed to fit back in the bottles)

Six-Pack of Poppy-Seed Dressing

MAKES 6 BOTTLES; 1 GIFT

This simple, sophisticated salad dressing is practically child's play. Just put all of the ingredients in a blender, then pour into empty Perrier bottles.

1 cup seedless raspberry preserves

1/3 cup honey

1 cup red wine or raspberry vinegar

1/2 cup lemon juice

1 1/2 cups vegetable oil

1 Tablespoon poppy seeds

1 teaspoon salt

Combine ingredients in blender jar. Blend about 40 seconds, or until dressing has creamy pink appearance.

Six-Pack of Perrier

6 washed and dried 6-ounce Perrier bottles
6 clean corks
6-pack carton from Perrier
3 twelve-inch pieces green curling ribbon
3 × 5-inch unruled index card
Green felt-tip marker
Hole punch

Use funnel to fill bottles, allowing room at top for corks. Push corks firmly into bottles. Place bottles in carton. Hold 3 strands ribbon together and tie through carton handle in knot. Fold card in half with crease at top. On front of card write in green marker:

"From source (your name)"

Inside card write:

*"To Add a Splash of Sparkle on
Your Favorite Fruit Salad"*

Punch hole in corner of card. Thread ribbon through hole and knot with another ribbon streamer. Curl all ribbon streamers with scissors.

◆◆◆

Vermont-Style Maple Bacon Salad Dressing

(Alison's House Dressing)

MAKES 1 GIFT

I once pleaded with a chef for this recipe after becoming "addicted" to his spinach salad. He was kind enough to share it with me. Soon, I was serving it to friends and evoking the same reaction. Some wanted the recipe; others begged me to bottle it and go into the salad dressing business. Since I have no intention of competing with Paul Newman, Alison's House Dressing will have to remain my most requested personal gift.

8 slices bacon

Olive oil (optional)

2/3 cup chopped Bermuda onions

1 clove garlic, crushed

1/2 cup red wine vinegar

1/2 cup maple syrup

1/4 teaspoon salt

1 cup mayonnaise (regular or reduced fat)

2 Tablespoons minced chives
(1 tablespoon dried chives)

Cut bacon into 1-inch pieces. Stir-fry bacon in large saucepan until extremely crisp and brown. All fat should be rendered out. Remove bacon bits with slotted spoon; drain on paper towels. Pour bacon drippings into a glass measuring cup. If necessary, add enough olive oil to bring the level up to $1/2$ cup.

Pour drippings back into saucepan, adding onions and garlic. Saute until onions are transparent. Remove saucepan from heat and pour in vinegar. Add maple syrup. Over low heat blend mixture with wire whisk until warm. Whisk in salt, mayonnaise, and chives until smooth and blended. Remove from heat.

Note: This dressing should be bottled while warm and stored in the refrigerator at all times. Recipe can easily be doubled or tripled.

If you are concerned about saturated fat, you may discard the drippings and substitute all of it with $1/2$ cup of olive oil. However, some of the wonderful flavor will be lost.

Mrs. Butterworth's™ Syrup Bottle

1 empty bottle Mrs. Butterworth's™
maple syrup without label
$1/4$ yard small check brown gingham fabric
Felt tip fabric marker

Fill bottle with dressing using funnel for easy pouring. Screw on cap. Wash and dry outside of bottle and cap. From gingham, cut: a 7-inch square, a 4 × 10-inch strip, and a $1 1/2$ × 15-inch strip. Fold 7-inch square diagonally into a triangle and press. Fold 4 × 10-inch strip in half to a 4 × 5-inch rectangle. Press with fold at top. Fold $1 1/2$ × 15-inch strip in half, lengthwise to a $3/4$ × 15-inch band, press.

Tie triangle bandana-style over bottle cap, tucking pointed end under tied ends at back of bottle's head. On the 4 × 5-inch fabric, fold back top layer (which will be the apron front). On the inside write with marker on lower half of fabric the following:

"(your name)'s House Dressing"
Heat and serve warm over
spinach salad. Top with seedless
red grapes, chopped apple,
raisins, and toasted walnuts

Tie apron around bottle by slipping folded edge of 15-inch band under folded edge of 4 × 5-inch rectangle. With apron centered on band, tie around waist, with bow at back of bottle.

Homemade Fruit and Herb Vinegars

MAKES 3 GIFTS OF 2 VINEGARS EACH

The world has discovered the wonders of flavored vinegar as a meat marinade, glaze for poultry, or to add a sparkle to salad dressing. Although flavored vinegars take only minutes to make, allow several weeks for flavors to mellow. Use empty wine bottles or purchase decorative decanters from a kitchen shop.

Berry Vinegar

3 cups fresh raspberries or blueberries, washed and drained

3 sixteen-ounce wine bottles or decanters

2 cups white vinegar

2 cups red wine vinegar

2 cups red wine

¼ cup honey

3 corks

Drop 1 cup berries into each bottle. Combine vinegars, wine, and honey in large saucepan. Bring to a simmer. Remove from heat. Pour mixture into bottles using a funnel. Cork bottles and allow flavors to blend for 2 to 4 weeks.

Sherry-Herb Vinegar

3 large sprigs fresh thyme
3 large sprigs fresh rosemary
3 large sprigs fresh sage
3 sixteen-ounce wine bottles or decanters
3 cups white vinegar
2 cups cider vinegar
1 cup dry golden sherry
3 corks

Divide herbs evenly, sticking a sprig of each into each bottle. Combine vinegars and sherry in large saucepan. Bring to simmer and remove from heat. Pour mixture into bottles using funnel. Cork bottles and allow flavors to blend for 2 to 4 weeks.

Recipe Gift Cards

Spray mount adhesive
3 three × five-inch unruled white index cards
1/4 yard glazed small-print chintz fabric
X-Acto knife
Hole punch
Felt-tip marker (coordinate to fabric color)
3 eight-inch lengths of 1/4-inch satin ribbon
coordinated to fabric color

Spray one side of each card with adhesive and press down to wrong side of fabric. Turn fabric over and smooth out any creases or lumps.

Trim fabric to edge of cards with X-Acto knife. Fold cards in half with fabric on outside. Punch hole through both sides, near upper left corner. Open cards and write appropriate recipe for the type of vinegar. Close cards, thread ribbon through each hole, and tie around neck of each bottle.

Berry Glazed Chops

4 four-ounce pork or veal chops

1 cup berry vinegar (reserve 1/2 cup)

1 Tablespoon butter

Wild rice

In nonreactive bowl, marinade chops overnight in 1/2 cup vinegar. Discard vinegar. Melt butter in skillet and brown chops on both sides. Add remaining 1/2 cup vinegar to saucepan and simmer with chops until reduced to a syrupy glaze. Serve with wild rice.

Golden-Glow Vinegrette

1 Tablespoon prepared mustard

1/3 cup sherry-herb vinegar

1/3 cup olive oil

2/3 cup vegetable oil

1/2 teaspoon salt

1/4 teaspoon cracked pepper

Combine ingredients in blender; blend until smooth and creamy. Keep refrigerated.

◆◆◆

Safari Sauce

MAKES THREE 8-OUNCE JARS

This is a simple sandwich sauce, assembled from supermarket condiments. It should be kept refrigerated by you and the recipient.

8-ounce jar of mango chutney

1 cup mayonnaise

$1/2$ cup prepared mustard

$1/2$ cup honey

2 teaspoons curry powder

Dash hot pepper sauce

Spoon chutney into mixing bowl and cut up any large chunks of fruit in the chutney. With wire whisk, blend in mayonnaise. Add mustard, honey, curry powder, and hot pepper sauce. Blend until thoroughly combined. Spoon into three 8-ounce jars and seal with lids.

Jungle-Jar Tops

$1/4$ yard tiger, leopard, or zebra print cotton fabric

Rubber bands

1 yard black cord

Use pinking shears to cut fabric into three 8-inch circles. Center circles over top of each jar, and slip rubber bands over fabric, gathering fabric around jar neck. Cut cord into three 12-inch lengths. Tie cord around each jar lid. Remove rubber bands.

Apple Orchard Barbecue Sauce

MAKES TWO 1-PINT GIFT JARS

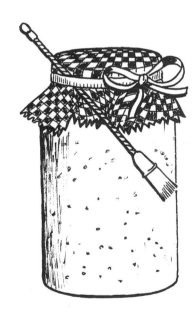

Before moving East, I grew up in barbecue country. Kansas City is one of the nation's sparerib capitals, and the perfect sauce is always debated. Some like it hot; some like it sweet; some like it smoky. I personally like them all. The appropriate sauce simply has to suit the sparerib. To me, the best sauce complements all types of ribs. Mildly sweet and smoky, it doesn't leave your forehead in a sweat. I used to make the sauce with cider from the Connett orchards (a family farm on my father's side). I now buy my cider from Connecticut country farmstands. And East Coast apples work well in a Midwestern BBQ sauce.

1 medium onion, grated or finely chopped

4 cups pressed apple cider
(not pasteurized apple juice)

1/2 cup cider vinegar

1/2 cup firmly packed dark brown sugar

1 Tablespoon whole mustard seed

1 teaspoon celery salt or celery seed

1 Tablespoon Worcestershire sauce

1 Tablespoon liquid smoke

2 twelve-ounce bottles chili sauce

Hot pepper sauce to taste (optional)

Bring ingredients to boil in large saucepan. Reduce heat and simmer until sauce is thickened and volume is halved. Pour hot sauce into two 1-pint sterilized jars. Seal with 2 pieced sterilized lids. Water-bath process for 10 minutes. Remove with tongs. Cool.

Opposite: Apple Orchard BBQ Sauce

Baster Brush Wrap

2 six-inch squares red-checked gingham fabric, cut with
pinking shears

Rubber bands
2 12-inch lengths ¼-inch wide red grosgrain ribbon
2 small baster brushes

Center gingham squares on jar lids. Slip rubber bands over fabric,
gathering in around the rim of jar. Tightly tie ribbon around each jar
lid. Tie ribbon streamers in bow around handle of each basting
brush. Remove rubber bands.

Opposite: Safari Sauce, page 69
Watermelon Rind Relish, page 72

Watermelon Rind Relish

MAKES 8 GIFT JARS

Watermelon is truly one of the joys of summer. By pickling watermelon, you can enjoy this treat year-round.

7 pounds watermelon rind

1 Tablespoon salt

6 lemons

4 oranges

3 cups granulated sugar

3 cups firmly packed light brown sugar

6 whole peppercorns

4 teaspoons whole cloves

1 quart apple cider vinegar

1 cup water

1/2 pound candied ginger, chopped
(or use 4-ounces each of candied ginger
and candied orange peel)

8 whole grape leaves
(optional—these help keep relish crisp)

8 cinnamon sticks

Peel off outer green skin of watermelon rind. Leave a scant amount of pink flesh attached. With a chef's knife dice into 1/4-inch cubes. Place rind in very large saucepan. Cover with water and bring to boil. Reduce heat and simmer until crisp-tender. Drain and transfer to bowl of ice water to stop the cooking. Drain rind well and pat dry with paper towels.

72

Cut lemon and orange rinds into strips and remove pits. Squeeze juice from lemons and oranges and reserve. Put citrus strips in large saucepan. Cover with cold water. Bring to a boil and boil 3 minutes. Remove rind with slotted spoon and discard water. Repeat process two more times to remove bitterness.

In large saucepan mix sugars. Add cinnamon, peppercorns, cloves, vinegar, water, ginger, lemon, and orange juice. Simmer 30 minutes, at medium heat, until reduced and slightly syrupy. Strain through a sieve to remove spices. Return liquid to saucepan adding watermelon rind and citrus strips. Simmer gently for about 30 minutes, or until watermelon rind appears translucent.

Meanwhile sterilize eight 1-pint jars. Place grape leaf in bottom of each. Remove fruit from syrup with slotted spoon and spoon into jars. Cook remaining syrup until slightly thickened and pour over fruit. Seal jars with sterilized two-piece lids. Water-bath process for 15 minutes. Remove jars with tongs. Cool.

Melon Slice Jar Tops

9 × 12-inch piece green felt

9 × 12-inch piece white felt

9 × 12-inch piece dark pink felt

Fabric glue

6 dozen tiny black shoe buttons

8 eight-inch circles, cut from dark pink gingham fabric with pinking shears

Rubber bands

2 yards ¼-inch wide green satin ribbon

Fig. 1

Cut 8 circles from green felt (using jar top as pattern, to fit lid). Cut 8 circles from white felt that are 3/4-inch smaller in diameter than green circles. Cut 8 circles from pink felt that are 3/4-inch smaller in diameter than white circles. Using fabric glue attach 9 buttons on pink felt to resemble watermelon seeds. Glue pink felt circles in center of white felt circles, then glue white felt in center of green felt circles (Fig. 1). Center pink gingham over tops of jars and slip rubber band over fabric and lid, gathering fabric around jar necks. Cut ribbon into 9-inch lengths and tie around jar necks. Remove rubber bands. Glue felt watermelon slices to gingham on jar tops.

◆◆◆

Swiss Chocolate Sundae Sauce

MAKES 2 JARS; 1 GIFT

Pour it over ice cream, and it's called coupe Toblerone™. Pour it into a ceramic pot and it's called chocolate fondue. This is a great dipping sauce for fruit, cookies, and cake.

4 three-ounce Toblerone™ milk chocolate honey almond-nougat bars

3/4 cup light cream

1 to 2 Tablespoons Creme de Cocao, Creme de Menthe, Khalua, Grand Marnier™, Chambord™, or Frangelico™

Break up chocolate and combine with cream in heavy-bottomed saucepan. Melt over low heat, stirring until creamy and smooth. Remove from heat. Pour into 2 sterilized 12-ounce jars. Seal with two-piece sterilized lids. Water-bath process for 5 minutes. Remove from kettle with tongs. Cool.

Chocolate Wrapper Wrap

2 six-inch circles of red dotted
Swiss cotton fabric
Rubber bands
2 twelve-inch lengths of Swiss-style
embroidered ribbon
Chocolate fondue pot with
dipping fork set (optional)

Center fabric circles over each jar lid, and slip rubber band over fabric, securing it around jar lid. Tightly knot ribbons around jar just under rubber bands. Remove rubber bands. Tie ends of ribbon in bows. If desired, present jars in fondue pot with dipping fork set.

SPECIAL GIFTS FOR SPECIAL PEOPLE

Green Thumb Gardener's Set
Cordon Bleu Chef's Hat
Beefy Home Baked Dog-Bone Biscuits
Couch Cats
Peanut Butter Birdseed Balls
Sports Nuts
Sneaker Sachets
Golf-Tee Topiary Tree
Plants for Problem Places
Planting Ideas
Quick-Fix Gifts for Special People

◆

Special Gifts for Special People

Special-interest gifts are tailored to the individual with a passion, from a sport or hobby to a favorite pet. Ironically, what should make it easier to shop for enthusiasts often makes it more difficult. They seem to have everything. The Wednesday golfer, weekend skier, or Monday-night football fan is probably a self-proclaimed pro. If you're not, it's hard to know what to give.

That's why many of the projects in this section are gag gifts. They'll always hit the spot.

Green Thumb Gardener's Set

MAKES 1 GIFT

An industry has evolved around selling upscale gardeners' gifts and gadgets. However, you can put together your own customized set of gardening tools and gadgets from the hardware store to make an impressive gift. Sponge painting the equipment is a good project for kids.

Drop cloth and aluminum foil

*1 large metal watering can with wide opening
(pre-painted can saves time)*

12-inch garden trowel with wooden handle

Plastic wrap

Masking tape

White or cream-colored spray paint

Leaf-green acrylic paint suitable for fabrics

Metal pie plate

Natural sponge

Paintbrush

*Garden gloves in white or cream
to match watering can*

Cover work surface with drop cloth or foil. Place watering can on surface. Stuff inside with foil to protect it from paint. Cover metal parts of trowel with plastic wrap, securing at handle with masking tape. If can and trowel are unpainted, give can and trowel handle 2 or 3 coats white paint. Dry between coats.

Pour green paint into pie plate. Pat paint with sponge, then stamp all over can and trowel handle to give marbled effect. Dry. With paintbrush, write: (recipient's name) Green Thumb on can with green paint. Paint one thumb of one garden glove, green.

Garden Set

Seed packets
2 yards green cellophane
Rubber band
1 1/2 yards wide green grosgrain ribbon
Cluster of dried flowers (optional)

Arrange trowel, gloves, and seeds to sit in watering can opening. Spread cellophane on table and place can in center. Bring cellophane up around sides of can, gathering into tassel at top. Secure tassel in place with rubber band. Tie green ribbon into bow around tassel. Tie bow around flowers. Remove rubber band. Trim edges of tassel with pinking shears.

Cordon Bleu Chef's Hat

MAKES 1 GIFT

A chef's hat, or toque, is guaranteed to bring a smile to the face of an amateur or professional cook. Several of my friends are chef-owners of their own restaurants and this gift got an amusing reaction.

12 inches 1-inch thick blue or red, white, and blue striped grosgrain ribbon

Fray check

1 cotton chef's toque (available from restaurant supply or cookware shop)

1-inch to 1 1/2-inch gold-metal button with crest or shield

Blue felt-tip fabric pen

Trim edges of ribbon, diagonally, with scissors. Put a few drops of fray check on edges to prevent unraveling. Fold ribbon in inverted V formation (Fig. 1). Press crease with iron. Stitch fold of ribbon to one side of hat, in middle of the band. Sew button securely on top of ribbon fold. With fabric pen, write one of following on band:

(name) the Great!

(name) the Magnifique!

Fig. 1

Bon Appétit Box

White tissue paper

1 white shirt box

*Page from food section of newspaper
including recipes and photos*

*2 yards 1/2-inch or 3/4-inch wide ribbon
to match ribbon on chef's hat*

Small wire whisk

Neatly wrap hat in several sheets white tissue. Put in shirt box.
Iron newspaper on low setting so ink doesn't rub off. Wrap box in
newspaper. Tie ribbon around box, by catching two opposite corners.
Make a bow with wire whisk slipped into it.

Beefy Home Baked Dog-Bone Biscuits

MAKES 2 DOZEN BISCUITS; 1 GIFT

This great gift for dog lovers also happens to be a popular birthday present at my house. I have nine dogs!

3 eggs

3 Tablespoons soy flour

3 Tablespoons wheat germ

3 Tablespoons nonfat dry milk powder

*3 beef bouillon cubes dissolved in
6 Tablespoons hot water*

1 Tablespoon Worcestershire sauce

3 cups whole wheat flour

Preheat oven to 350°F (175°C).

Beat eggs slightly in large mixing bowl. Stir in soy flour, wheat germ, dry milk, bouillon, and Worcestershire. Add flour and work into a stiff, crumbly dough with your hands.

Divide dough into two balls. Divide each ball into 12 pieces.
Pat each piece into a 3-inch rectangle, 1/2-inch thick, on ungreased cookie sheet. Using biscuit cutter or knife, trim to shape of dog bone.

Bake 25 minutes. Turn biscuits over with a spatula and bake 25 minutes longer.

Personalized Dog Dish

Acrylic paint
Double-sided plastic dog dish
Sheet of transparent rainbow Mylar tissue
2 feet curling ribbon in color to match paint
Scissors

Paint dog's name across front of dish. Dry. Pile about a dozen bones in each side of dish. Wrap Mylar tissue around dish lengthwise, taping seam underneath. Cut ribbon in half. Tie each end with piece of ribbon. Curl streamers.

Note: For large dogs, you could use one big ceramic bowl.

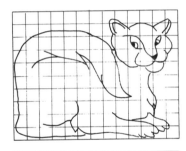

Couch Cats

MAKES 2 GIFT PILLOWS

Couch cats make a purrfect pair of pillows for feline-loving friends. Cut from cotton muslin and drawn with fabric markers, these only require basic sewing skills.

Brown paper

Black felt-tip marker

1 1/2 yards unbleached muslin

Black plus yellow, green, or blue felt-tip fabric markers

Cream-colored thread

Fiberfill (about 4 pounds)

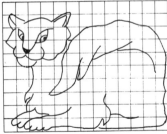

1 Square = 1 Inch

Using black felt-tip marker, enlarge cat patterns (14 inches × 18 inches) onto brown paper. Draw a 1 1/2-inch seam around cats. Cut out patterns. Fold fabric in half so that it's 24 inches × 54 inches. Place patterns on fabric. Cut from fabric so you'll have front and back for each pillow.

For pillow fronts, slip cat drawing under muslin. Pin in place. Gently trace pattern showing through, using smooth even strokes, with black fabric marker. Fill in eyes with colored marker. If necessary, iron fabric on low setting to set markings. Pin wrong sides of pillows together (artwork facing in).

With sewing machine, use cream-colored thread to stitch around pillows allowing 1/2-inch seam. Leave 8-inch opening at bottom of each pillow. Turn pillows right-side out, and stuff with fiberfill. Slip stitch bottom opening.

Bell Bow

8 sheets tissue paper in one color

2 twelve-inch pieces heavy gauge yarn
gift tie in contrasting color

2 large jingle bells

For each pillow, lay out doubled sheet of tissue paper, placing another doubled sheet of tissue crosswise. Stand pillow in center bringing sides up around it. Gather tissue in tassel at top. Tie with piece of yarn. Thread bell onto yarn and tie in bow. Trim edges of tassel with pinking shears.

Peanut Butter Birdseed Balls

MAKES 8 TO 12 BALLS

Bird lovers love to feed their feathered friends, so they can watch them from their windows. Since I started cooking for the flock, we've acquired an aviary of interesting species. It's always a joy to be visited by a beautiful cardinal while having breakfast. But the big surprise came a few years ago—bright green parrots. It's rumored they escaped from a boat near Black Rock harbor in my part of Connecticut. Now they've multiplied into a huge colony, and bird watchers, armed with binoculars, are always roaming our street.

¹/₂ pound ground-beef suet

1 cup creamy peanut butter

2 cups cornmeal

Decorative cord

Wild birdseed, hulled or unhulled sunflower seeds, barberries, or dried red and blue corn kernels

In large saucepan over low heat, melt suet, stirring occasionally. Strain rendered suet into large bowl, discarding crisp particles. Blend in peanut butter and cornmeal to make stiff dough. Chill mixture 30 minutes, until easily shaped with hands.

Meanwhile, cut about eight to twelve 14-inch lengths of cord. Tie ends of each together in knot making loops. Mold balls around knot on each loop, so that knot is in center. Pour one, or a combination, of suggested seeds into pie plate. Roll balls in seeds, to coat thoroughly. Refrigerate at least one hour, until firm.

Birdwatcher's Basket

3 yards 1-inch wide satin ribbon

Audubon magazine

Medium to large straw basket with handle

Bird tail feathers (find some on the ground,
or buy pheasant feathers from craft store)

Binoculars (optional)

Cut 12 inches from ribbon. Roll up magazine and tie bow around it. Cut remaining ribbon in half. Tie in bow at one side of basket handle's base. Wind streamers back and forth around handle. Tie bow at opposite side, catching feathers in ribbon. Arrange birdseed balls in basket along with magazine and binoculars.

Sports Nuts

MAKES 1 HELMET OR GLOVE GIFT

Homemade honey-roasted nuts are packaged in the appropriate sporting gear for a favorite fan. If you're in a hurry, put Cracker Jacks™ or a jar of nuts in the present.

1 egg white, slightly beaten

1 teaspoon cider vinegar

2 Tablespoons honey

8-ounce jar dry roasted peanuts (1 ²/₃ cups)

¹/₂ cup whole unblanched almonds

¹/₂ cup pecan halves

²/₃ cup sugar

¹/₄ teaspoon cinnamon

³/₄ teaspoon salt

Preheat oven to 300°F (150°C).

Combine egg white, vinegar, and honey in a bowl. Toss with nuts to coat. Combine sugar, cinnamon, and salt in a small bowl. Add to nuts and toss until they're evenly coated with sugar. Spread nuts out on buttered cookie sheet. Bake 20 to 25 minutes. Spread nuts on sheet of foil and cool. Break into small clusters.

Football Nut

Child's football helmet or stadium cap
2 yards cellophane, clear or in a team color
Tickets to a game
Rubber band
2 twelve-inch lengths of ¼-inch wide
satin ribbon in team colors

Turn helmet upside down. Cut cellophane in half and line inside of helmet with a sheet. Fill helmet with nuts. Place helmet on second sheet of cellophane, and bring sides up around helmet. Gather cellophane together at top, slipping tickets in between layers. Secure cellophane in tassel with rubber band. Trim tassel to 3 inches with pinking shears. Tie ribbons in bow, just underneath rubber band. Remove rubber band.

Baseball Nut

Package nuts in same manner as football helmet, using baseball mitt. Slip baseball cards into package.

Sneaker Sachets

MAKES 2 SACHETS; 1 GIFT

For a marathon runner, race walker, tennis pro, or even an aerobics class dropout, this is an ideal gift. For women, use a floral-scented potpourri. For men, try a spice or cedar scent.

1/8 yard (4 1/2 inches)
(women's sachet: glazed floral chintz
or candy stripe fabric)

(men's sachet: foulard necktie print
or classic plaid fabric)

Coordinating thread

Puff paint in color to coordinate
or contrast with fabric

12 inches of 1/4-inch wide satin ribbon
in color to coordinate with fabric

2 to 3 cups potpourri

Fig.1

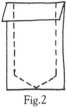

Fig.2

Fig.3

Cut two 4 × 15-inch strips from fabric. Fold strips in half, right sides together so they measure 4 × 7 1/2 inches (Fig. 1). Fold back top edges of fabric 1 1/2 inches and mark dots 1 1/2 inches from fold, on both sides (Fig. 2). Stitch as shown, with 1/2-inch seams at sides (Fig. 3). Trim corners and side seams to 1/4 inch with pinking shears. Turn right-side out.

At toes of sachets, write or print monogram initials with puff paint. Dry thoroughly. Follow manufacturer's directions for pressing puff paint with iron. Stuff sachet with potpourri to within 1 1/2 inches from edges. Sew across top, within 3/4 inch from edge. Cut ribbon in half and tack center of ribbon in center of top seam of sachet. Tie ribbon in bows.

Sock Wrap

*2 sheets tissue paper in color to
coordinate with sachets*

1 pair athletic socks

*1/2 yard 1/4-inch wide ribbon
in same color as sachets*

Wrap each sachet by centering on piece of tissue paper. Gather
edges around it. Stuff, toe-side down into socks, with loose tissue
sticking out from ankles of socks. Fold cuffs down on socks.
Cut ribbon in half and tie one around center of each sock cuff.
Tie ribbons in bows and, if desired, tie socks together with streamer
from each ribbon.

Sock Wrap

Golf-Tee Topiary Tree

MAKES 1 TREE GIFT

There's something about a golf ball, sitting on a tee, that has always reminded me of a topiary tree. It seems only "logical" that they must grow on them: The tree buds with tees, then bares golf balls. When the balls are ripe, they fall to the ground and grow into more topiary trees.

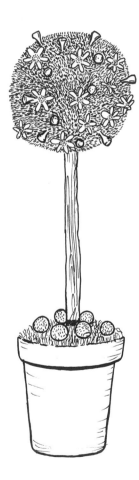

5-inch Styrofoam ball

*15-inch long, 1-inch thick straight stick
from tree branch*

Cube of Styrofoam oasis or floral foam

*Flowerpot 4 1/2 inches high,
6 1/2 inches wide*

Hot glue gun

4 to 6 small rocks

Stapler or floral pins

Spanish moss (sheet-style)

2 dozen golf tees in one color

Dried flowers

Eucalyptus leaves

Florist's grass

7 to 10 golf balls

Make a hole in bottom of Styrofoam ball, and insert stick halfway through. Remove stick from ball. Cut a piece of Styrofoam cube that will fit into 2 1/2 inch high pot and is wide enough to touch inner edges of pot. Glue foam to bottom of pot. Poke stick all the

94

way down into cube and remove. Coat stick end with hot glue, and insert into hole. Glue rocks to foam around base of stick for balance. Staple or pin moss on Styrofoam ball. Stick golf tees evenly around ball.

Trim stems from flowers and leaves. With hot glue gun, attach them to ball, distributing evenly. Coat top of stick with hot glue, and slip ball onto stick through original hole. Cover rocks and foam, at the base, with nest of florist's grass. Secure to rocks with glue. Arrange 7 to 10 golf balls around base of tree, as if they've "dropped off."

Sock Bow

2 yards of clear cellophane
Rubber band
1 lightweight knit argyle knee sock

Lay sheet of cellophane out on table. Place tree in center. Bring cellophane up around sides of tree and gather in tassel at top. Secure in place with rubber band. Tie sock around rubber band concealing it.

Note: This makes a very practical "gag" gift. The golfer can always "harvest" the balls in the pot for a game.

Plants for Problem Places

Everyone loves a healthy plant, but one that quickly dies makes a depressing gift. Before choosing a plant gift, visualize the environment that the plant will be living in. If you know it's going to a windowless hospital room or office, plan accordingly. Not all plants thrive in sunshine. Some drown in plentiful water while others flourish in a steamy bathroom. Many plants die because they're either ill-suited to their surroundings, or they simply don't come with a care label. Here are some suggestions for placing plants in problem places, along with care and feeding instructions (important to include on any card).

Shady Spot, Low Light Plants
(can be placed as far as 3 yards away from a window)

Best Bets: Kentia palm

Warneckei dracaena

cut-leaf philodendron

flowering peace lily

TLC Tips: Pinch off new leaves growing from tops of stems, to prevent from growing too long. Fertilize soil only once a year.

Dark Nook, No Natural Light Needed, Plants
(for windowless rooms and offices)

Best Bets: *Chinese evergreen*

dwarf parlor palm

heart-leaf philodendron

golden pothos

snake plant

bird's nest sansevieria
(for small nooks)

TLC Tips: Water plants only after soil becomes dry. Dust inhibits growth, so clean monthly with a moist sponge. If plants fail to thrive, move into a lighter spot for a few weeks.

Arid Room Plants
(for dry, hot spots with surplus sun)

Best Bets: *jade plant*

crown of thorns

variegated agave

most cacti

TLC Tips: Water only when necessary. Jars of water placed around plant help plant absorb its own moisture through evaporation. Test for dryness by poking finger 2" into soil.

Cascading Plants
(good for semi-shaded corners with indirect light)

Best Bets: arrowhead vine

asparagus fern

spider plant

TLC Tips: Resist temptation to polish shiny leaf with oil or furniture wax. Clean with damp sponge monthly. Brown leaf tips may be trimmed with scissors.

Hearty Plants for Cool Environments
(ideal in cool, drafty environments ranging from 65° to 45° in a 24 hour period)

Best Bets: English ivy

Japanese fatsia

Calamondin orange

piggy-back plant

Christmas cactus

TLC Tips: Keep in air conditioning during summer months. Shade from intense mid-day sun with curtain. Avoid direct contact with cold window panes during winter. Water when soil is dry, 1" from surface.

High Humidity Tropical Plants
(ideal in bathrooms with showers)

Best Bets: *African violets*
prayer plant
Boston fern
silver-nerved fitlonia
bird's-nest fern
brake ferns

TLC Tips: Never over-water plants living in high humidity. Do not fertilize African violets while in resting cycle. Use tepid (never cold) water for watering. These plants thrive under fluorescent lighting.

◆◆◆

Planting Ideas

Plants as presents need little, or no, packaging, although you may want to create your own customized wrap. Here are some suggestions:

Chintz or Burlap Wrap

Trim foil supplied by florist down to rim of pot. Cut circle of glazed chintz or colored burlap to a diameter equal to the width of the pot plus 3 times its height. Place plant in center of circle and bring fabric up around sides of plant. Secure fabric in place with ribbon or cord around rim.

Sponge-Painted Pot

If repotting choose pot the same size, or slightly larger than the plant's. Otherwise, select a pot that the plant's pot can easily sit in. Use one or two colors ceramic paints and natural sponge to create marble-like design. Pour paint into metal pie plates and lightly sponge-print, using one color at a time, on the pot. Dry thoroughly.

Quick-Fix Gifts for Special People

Swiss Sweets for Super Skier: Fill a knitted ski cap with assorted Swiss chocolate bars such as Toblerone or Lindt. Add a bag of toasted hazelnuts. Tie the opening of the hat with a pair of matching mittens strung together.

Beach-Bum Bag for the Sun Worshipper: Fill a canvas tote with sunscreen, lip balm, moisturizer, sun visor, a good novel, and a bottle of mineral water.

Wilderness-Survival Kit for Campers, Hunters, Hikers, and Mountain Bikers: Fill a picnic basket or small ice chest with granola bars and freeze-dried food. Include a map and a compass with a card that says, "In case you get lost."

Fisherman's Bait for the Angler: Fill a fishing creel with gold-fish bowl bites (see Hospitality Treats) or your fisherman's favorite snack food.

Car Buff Care Box: Fill toolbox or chest with tire gauge, window scraper, window-washer fluid, quart of oil, antifreeze, car wax, chamois cloths, flashlight, flares, road atlas, or even air freshners. Tie a toy car to the handle.

Power-Lunch Box for Office Buddy: Paint "Power Lunch" on a child's lunch box. Replace Thermos with a split of Champagne, and enclose a gift certificate to a favorite restaurant.

Super Tote for the Shopoholic: Write "Shop Till You Drop!" in gold-glitter paint on a bright colored shopping bag. Fill with play money. In a special envelope, enclose real coupons or gift certificates to favorite stores.

Music Lover's Custom Cassette: Tape a collection of your friend's favorite songs. Then make a personalized label. Wrap the cassette in a cover page from Rolling Stone Magazine or a page of sheet music.

Beach Bum Bag for the Sun Worshipper

Car Buff Care Box

Power Lunch Box

Music Lover's Custom Cassette

Tightwad's Penny-Pincher Bank: A gentle joke for the compulsively thrifty is to create a bank from a beverage can with a tab opening. Use a hot glue gun to completely cover the can with newly minted pennies.

Secretary's Queen-for-a-Day Kit: For a birthday or Secretary's Day, surprise her with a bouquet of roses, a dime-store tiara and a satin-ribbon sash (like the kind Miss America wears) that says: "Queen for a Day."

Opposite: Green Thumb Gardener's Set, page 80
Sponge Painted Pots, page 100

5

GIFTS FOR KIDS

Designer Sneaker Set

Frog Prince Pillow

Cedar Closet Snakes

Checkerboard Cookie Box

Molasses Monkeys in Banana Bags

Peanut Butter Apples

♦

Opposite: Peanut Butter Bird Seed Balls, page 88

Gifts for Kids

In an age when Saturday morning TV creates an insatiable appetite for toys that don't last, it's nice to make something special. It probably won't break the same day, but if it's edible it will be eaten within two hours. It might even stimulate the imagination.

With most of these projects kids get hands-on involvement in making gifts for friends. They'll learn new skills in either the preparation or the play. No matter how old children are, chances are there's something they can get involved with, even if it's just scribbling on some wrapping paper, or shaping cookie dough. Exposing children to the joy of giving helps get rid of the "Gimmies!"

Designer Sneaker Set

MAKES 1 GIFT

Expensive athletic shoes have become every parent's nightmare. But you needn't spend a fortune for a child to feel like a million bucks. Let children customize their own shoes and be trendsetters.

1 pair white or colored athletic socks

Assorted felt-tip fabric markers

Glitter paint in writing tubes in 4 colors

Tacky fabric glue

Package of sequins

*Assorted colors plastic buttons,
embroidery needle, and thread*

1 pair inexpensive white sneakers

Fill socks with craft materials and stuff into sneakers.

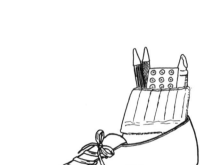

Customized Shoe Box

Aluminum foil

Shoe box

Black or deep-colored spray paint

Acrylic paint in 2 vivid colors

Paintbrush

2 sheets of tissue paper in colors
to match vivid paints

Pair of bright-colored shoe laces in color
to coordinate with one of paints

Spread work area with sheets of foil. Open box and place both lid and bottom so that inside faces down on foil. Cover with two coats of black spray paint, allowing paint to dry between coats.

Create a logo using initials, nickname, or contraction of names. For example, my name is Alison Boteler, so I might call my shoes "ALBO." Use brush and vivid-color paint to repeat logo on lid and sides of box using consistent lettering style. When paint is dry, line box with tissue paper and place shoes in box. Separate shoe laces and tie each one around width of box, about 2 inches from each end.

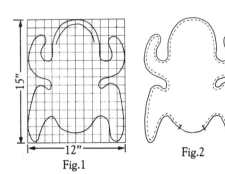

Frog Prince Pillow

MAKES 1 GIFT PILLOW

With some basic sewing skills you can whip up a fairy tale frog pillow. It makes an enchanting gift for a special little "sleeping beauty."

12 × 15-inch piece dark green felt

12 × 15-inch piece light green felt

2 1-inch yellow plastic buttons

Black embroidery wool

Fabric chalk

Green thread

Fiberfill (to stuff pillow)

Crown

(instructions follow)

15"

12"

Fig.1

Fig.2

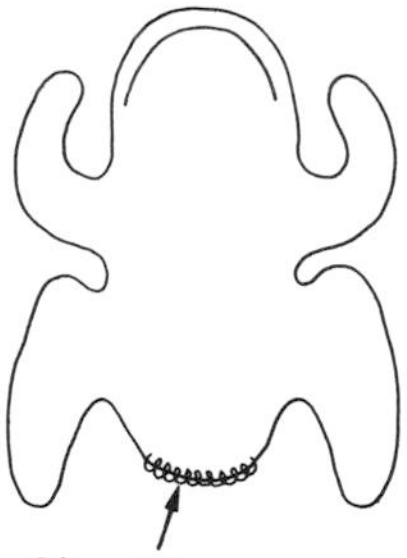

Slipstich

Fig.3

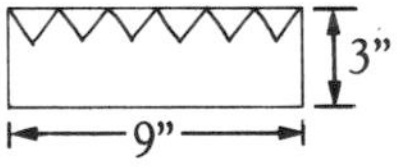

3"

9"

Fig.4

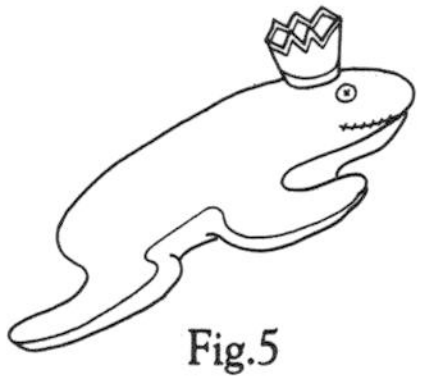

Fig.5

Draw a frog pattern on piece of brown paper so frog is about 12 × 15 inches (Fig. 1). Cut pattern out of both colors of felt. On dark green felt sew buttons on for eyes using black wool thread. Stitch through holes enough times so thread resembles a "pupil" in center of button "eye." Chain stitch black wool along mouth line, marked with fabric chalk. Place wrong sides of fabric together and stitch on sewing machine or by hand using green thread. Leave space for stuffing pillow (Fig. 2). Turn right-side out (Fig. 3). Stuff pillow with fiberfill and whipstitch closed.

Crown: Cut notches in a 3 × 9-inch strip of yellow felt to resemble a crown. Outline and decorate crown with tube of gold glitter fabric paint (Fig. 4). Whipstitch sides together and whipstitch crown to the top of frog's head (Fig. 5).

"Kiss-Me-Goodnight" Bag

Several sheets green tissue paper
Large plain brown grocery bag
Green crayon
12-inch piece 1-inch wide green grosgrain ribbon

Wrap frog in several layers of tissue. With green crayon write
"Kiss Me Goodnight!" all over grocery bag. Slide frog into bag.
Fold over edges of bag and place center of ribbon in center of folded
edge. Staple in place through layers of bag fold. Tie ribbon in a bow.

Cedar Closet Snakes

MAKES 2 SNAKES; 1 GIFT

This practical gift recycles Dad's old neckties into moth-repellent sweater protectors. These silly snakes hang around hangers and are a fun project for kids to make for their friends or fathers.

Scraps of red felt

Felt to match ties for diamond shapes

2 old neckties (stain free, the wider, the better)

Bag of cedar hamster-cage shavings

Package of 1/2-inch moveable plastic hobby eyes (sew-on type)

4 small black shoe buttons

Cut scraps of red felt into two strips about 3/4 inch wide, and 6 inches long. Make "V"-shaped notches in one end of each strip to resemble snake tongues (Fig. 1). Cut diamond-shaped felt pieces to cover large and small open ends to ties (Fig. 2). Stitch tongues to inside of large tie ends and slip-stitch diamonds onto open ends of ties.

At both ends of ties seams are left open for about 6 inches. Stuff ties with shavings through openings. Slip-stitch openings closed (Fig. 3). Stitch eyes onto large ends of ties. Stitch two shoe buttons on each tie for "nostrils" (Fig. 4).

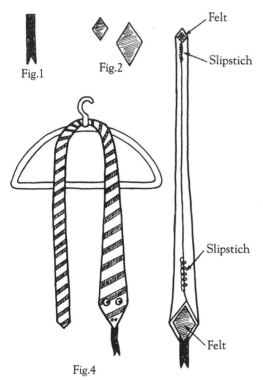

Fig.1

Fig.2

Felt

Slipstich

Slipstich

Felt

Fig.4

Fig.3

Snake Roll-Up Wrap

8 sheets of tissue paper
Curling ribbon

For each snake lay out 2 sheets of tissue paper. Top with 2 more
sheets. Grab narrower edge of top sheets and pull halfway off of
bottom sheets, so tissue overlaps in one long layer. Place snake at
lengthwise edge of wrap and roll up. Cut five 15-inch lengths of
curling ribbon and tie ends. Tie roll in middle, and halfway from
ends and middle. Don't tie tightly. Curl ribbon ends of all 5 sections
with scissors. Repeat with remaining snake and 4 sheets of tissue
paper.

◆◆◆

Checkerboard Cookie Box

MAKES 1 GIFT

Ordinary Oreo™ cookies become an uncommon treat when they're part of a checkerboard box. This is an ideal travel gift. It keeps kids occupied for hours on a plane, train, or car trip. It's also a snack that's easily replenished at every stop.

Tacky fabric glue and craft brush

2-piece cardboard gift box
(12-inch square, 1 inch deep)

12-inch square of red felt (cut to fit top lid)

1 1/4 yards of 1-inch wide red
or black grosgrain ribbon

Black fabric paint

Metal pie plate

1 1/2-inch square sponge

Apply glue with brush to top of box lid. Press felt onto lid, smoothing out lumps or wrinkles. Apply glue around sides of box lid and cover with ribbon. Pour paint into pie plate and pat sponge into paint. Stamp a checkerboard design onto felt, at 1 1/2-inch intervals and staggering rows (see checkerboard design). Dry thoroughly.

Checker Cookies

1 sheet red or black tissue paper

2 dozen Oreo cookies

2 dozen contrasting cookies
(use vanilla sandwich cookies)

1 yard, 1-inch wide black
or red grosgrain ribbon

Line bottom of box with doubled sheet of tissue paper. Arrange cookies in box so that each type is on one side. Fold tissue back over cookies and replace lid on box. Tie ribbon in a bow around box, catching opposite corners.

Note: 12 cookies are used by each player for a game of checkers. Part of the fun is eating your opponent's captured cookies. There are enough cookies in a box for two sets.

Molasses Monkeys in Banana Bags

MAKES 4 DOZEN COOKIES; 6 GIFTS

As a child, I called these molasses cookies "monkey faces." When raisins are baked into the soft ginger dough, the cookies come out of the oven with comical expressions, like little monkey faces. These are a great gift for children and the kind of project they can even make for their own friends.

$^{1}/_2$ cup butter-flavored shortening

1 cup firmly packed dark brown sugar

$^{1}/_2$ cup molasses

$^{1}/_2$ cup milk

1 teaspoon vinegar

2 $^{1}/_2$ cups all-purpose flour

1 teaspoon baking soda

$^{1}/_2$ teaspoon salt

$^{1}/_2$ teaspoon ginger

14 teaspoon nutmeg

1 teaspoon cinnamon

Raisins

4 dozen pecan halves

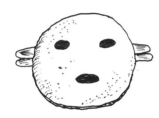

Fig.1

Preheat oven to 375°F (190°C).

Cream shortening, sugar, and molasses in mixing bowl. Blend in milk and vinegar. Combine flour, soda, salt, and spices in a separate bowl; blend into molasses mixture. Drop rounded teaspoonfuls of dough onto ungreased baking sheet. Place 3 raisins on each cookie (one for a mouth, two for eyes). Cut pecan halves in half across the middle. Insert pecan piece, cut side into dough, on each side of cookie for ears (Fig. 1).

Bake 10 to 12 minutes, or until set. Allow cookies to rest on baking sheet for about a minute, then lift off with spatula. Cool on wire rack.

Banana Bags

Yellow and dark brown crayons
6 brown paper lunch sacks
2 yards ½-inch wide yellow ribbon
Stapler

Outline banana shapes on sacks with brown crayon. Fill in bananas with yellow crayon adding characteristic bruises and speckles with brown crayon. Fill each bag with 8 cookies. Close bag. Fold closed twice in 1-inch folds. Cut ribbon into 12-inch lengths and staple each piece in the center of folded top. Tie ribbons in bows (Fig. 2).

Fig.2

Peanut Butter Apples

MAKES 1 DOZEN APPLES

Peanut butter and apples are a classic kid combination. Children love to help with dipping. Be sure to use a deep, narrow bowl for easier coating. These make a festive birthday party favor and fun activity.

2 twelve-ounce packages peanut-flavored chips

1/4 cup butter-flavored vegetable shortening

12 crisp, medium-sized apples

12 wooden popsicle sticks

1 1/2 cups roasted, chopped peanuts

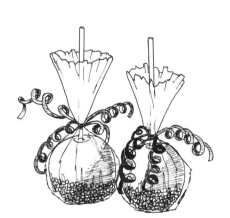

Combine peanut butter-flavored chips and shortening in a deep narrow heatproof glass or metal bowl. Heat hot plate on low heat. Place bowl on hot plate and melt mixture, stirring until smooth. Remove stems from apples and insert sticks halfway through. Dip apples into coating using spoon to help coat apples as necessary. Allow as much excess coating to drip off as possible.

Place peanuts in 1 or 2 shallow bowls. Immediately dip bottom of each apple in chopped peanuts. Place apples on foil or waxed paper-lined tray. Chill briefly to set coating.

Crystal Apple Wrap

12 twelve-inch squares of rainbow Mylar tissue
4 yards of 4 different colors of curling ribbon

Place each apple in center of Mylar tissue square. Cut ribbons into 12-inch lengths and divide into 12 sets, with every color included. Gather Mylar tissue around apples at base of stick. Hold ribbons together and tie around tissue at base of stick. Curl streamers of ribbon with scissors.

Note: For a dipping project involving several children, I recommend an electric hot plate. It's both simpler and safer than gathering a group of kids around a stovetop double boiler.

Opposite: *Frog Prince Pillow, page 108*
Cedar Closet Snakes, page 110

6

ANNUAL EVENTS AND HOLIDAY HOUSEWARMERS

Chambord Bonbons

Spring Chickens

Eggsquisite Easter Tree

"Super Mom" Custom T-Shirt

Toffee Bars in "Not Another Tie!" Box

Jumping Jack-O-Lanterns

Trick-or-Treat Halloween Wreath

Pumpkin Popcorn Balls

Maple-Leaf Cookies

Hanukkah Cutout Cookies

Crispy Christmas Trees

Nutcracker Christmas Wreath

Store-Bought Cookie Creations

Holiday Dressed-Up Doughnuts

Almost Edible Architecture

New Year's Buffet "Boar's" Head

Opposite: Molasses Monkeys in Banana Bags, page 114
Peanut Butter Apples, page 116

Annual Events and Holiday Housewarmers

◆◆

We tend to think of the official holidays as Thanksgiving and Christmas. However, holidays happen all year round. From February's Valentine's Day hearts and flowers to Fourth of July barbecues, we always need a gift to bring. Even annual events like Mother's Day and Father's Day are occasions that draw families together. What makes all of these celebrations so special are the people involved. That's why personalized gifts for these holidays are the most meaningful. No matter how hectic your life is, it takes amazingly little time to put together some of the projects in this section.

Holidays were made for children. The rituals associated with each holiday will someday become cherished emories. After all, that's how traditions are born. It's important to include children in holiday preparations. No matter how small the contribution may be, there are plenty of opportunities for little helping hands. Elements from all of these projects can be mastered by children. Making gift garlands, an eggsquisite egg tree, or jumping jack-o-lanterns is a rewarding way to spend quality time with your kids.

Chambord Bonbons

MAKES 1 GIFT

1 cup finely crushed vanilla wafers

1 cup powdered sugar

1 cup toasted chopped almonds

2 Tablespoons cocoa powder

2 Tablespoons butter

1/4 cup raspberry preserves

1/4 cup Chambord™ or raspberry liqueur

*6 ounces German or sweet baking chocolate,
grated or ground in food processor*

Combine vanilla wafers, powdered sugar, almonds, and cocoa powder in mixing bowl. Heat butter and raspberry preserves, just until butter melts. Blend into crumb mixture, along with Chambord. Chill one hour, then mold into about twenty to twenty-four 1-inch balls. Roll each ball in grated chocolate.

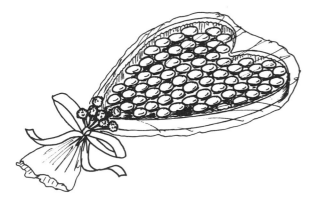

Heart Tray

9- or 10-inch paper doily
9- or 10-inch pink or red plastic heart-shaped tray
Large sheet rainbow Mylar tissue
32-inch square pink tulle fabric
Rubber band
12 inches each ¼-inch satin ribbon
in pink, white, lavender, or red, if using red tray
Dried baby's breath

Place doily in plastic tray. Arrange Chambord bonbons in tray. Lay sheet of Mylar tissue on tulle, centering if tulle is slightly larger. Place tray on Mylar, so that wide end of heart is in center. Fold Mylar with tulle over top of tray with edges meeting at bottom point. Gather tulle and Mylar tissue. Secure with rubber band. Hold all three ribbons and tie around tulle, just above rubber band. Remove rubber band. Trim tulle and tissue with pinking shears to a 3-inch tassel. Tie ribbons in bow, catching it around baby's breath.

Instant Gift

Purchase one or two roses with a vial at base to preserve freshness. Arrange rose(s) in a clear glass vase and fill with gold foil-wrapped chocolate Kisses™. Tie a gold wired ribbon into a bow around the vase.

 ◆◆◆

Spring Chickens

MAKES 2 DOZEN CANDIES; 2 EGG-CARTON GIFTS

Little lemon-coconut chicks are as much fun as a Play-Doh™ project. These are similar to marzipan candies, but less expensive to make. Place chickens in Easter baskets or individual egg carton nests.

3-ounce package lemon-flavored gelatin

14-ounce package (5 1/3 cups) flaked coconut

14-ounce can sweetened condensed milk

1 or 2 drops yellow gel food coloring (optional)

Toasted slivered almonds

Semisweet chocolate minichips

Combine gelatin, coconut, condensed milk, and food coloring in mixing bowl. Set aside 1/3 of mixture for heads. Mold remainder into 24 balls. Shape reserved mixture into 24 smaller balls for heads. Press small balls firmly on top of larger balls. Insert two almonds, one on top of the other, into each head for beaks. Use minichips for eyes.

Egg-Carton Nests

2 to 4 drops green gel food coloring
1 Tablespoon water
1-quart jar
2 cups shredded coconut
Bottom trays of 2 egg cartons
3 yards yellow cellophane, color to coordinate with egg carton
Green and yellow curling ribbon

Mix food coloring and water in jar. Add coconut and shake until evenly covered. Press a heaping tablespoon coconut into each cup of egg carton, building up around sides to create a nest. Set one chick in each nest. Allow chicks and nests to dry overnight, uncovered. Cut cellophane into two 1¹/₂-yard sheets. Wrap each tray in cellophane. Tie top in tassel with several strands of ribbon held together. Curl streamers with scissors. Trim tassels with pinking shears.

Eggsquisite Easter Tree

MAKES 2 DOZEN EGGS; 1 TREE GIFT

Easter egg trees have always been a tradition around our house. Give these sugar-coated eggs as a gift that can be reused every year. Store them in egg cartons.

Darning needle

*2 dozen raw eggs or plastic eggs
(from craft store)*

Craft brush

Tacky craft glue

Colored sugar
(instructions follow)

*2 yards each pink, blue, yellow and green
$1/8$-inch wide satin ribbon*

*24 nine-inch square pink, blue, yellow
and green tulle fabric*

*Branch with off-shoot branches
and twigs for hanging*

Gold or pastel spray paint

Hot glue gun or tacky craft glue

3 inch cube of oasis or floral foam

6 $1/2$-inch glass flower pot

*$1 1/2$ pounds pink, blue, yellow,
and green jelly beans*

Fig.1 .   Fig.2

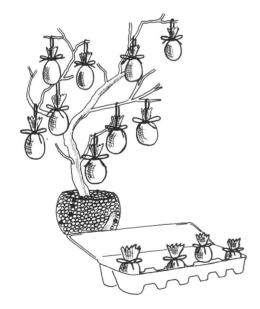

For raw eggs: pierce both ends of each egg with needle. Force contents of egg out through one end, by blowing into other end while leaning over a bowl. When eggs are empty, dry overnight.

Using dried eggs or plastic eggs, brush surface of each egg with tacky craft glue. Roll 6 eggs in each color sugar until completely coated. Allow to dry. Cut ribbon into 6 12-inch pieces. Fold ribbon in half and tie a knot, 3 inches from loop (Fig. 1). Match tulle to egg color. Gather tulle around each egg, with a tassel of tulle at small end. Tie matching or contrasting ribbon ends around tulle in secure bow (Fig. 2). To make tree spray paint branch with gold spray. Dry thoroughly.

Meanwhile, glue oasis to bottom of flowerpot with glue gun. Insert branch in oasis to make a hole. Remove and coat end with glue. Insert in oasis and alow to dry. Fill pot around oasis with jelly beans.

Colored sugar: Fill four 1-quart jars with 2 cups sugar. To each jar, add a few drops pink, blue, yellow or green gel food coloring. Shake jars until sugar is evenly colored. Pour sugar into 4 bowls.

Gilded Cartons

2 empty egg cartons

Aluminum foil

Gold or pastel spray paint

*1 yard ¼-inch wide pink, blue, yellow
or green satin ribbon*

*30-inch square pink, blue, yellow
or green tulle fabric*

Place open egg cartons upside-down on foil. Coat with gold spray paint. Dry thoroughly. Turn over and coat inside with spray paint. Dry thoroughly. Place tulle-wrapped eggs in cartons.

Cut ribbon into three 12-inch pieces. Tie one piece in a bow around the center of each carton. Place tree on top of tulle, so that bottom of pot is in center. Gather edges of tulle around base of tree and tie with remaining ribbon.

Note: Packaging eggs separately for the presentation prevents breakage in transit. It also allows children to decorate the tree themselves.

"Super Mom" Custom T-Shirt

MAKES 1 GIFT

Fabric crayons are truly a remarkable invention transforming "refrigerator art" into textile design. Simple crayon drawings are transferred onto T-shirts with an iron. This process is easier for young children than using fabric paints. Older children or adults should help with ironing.

Fabric crayons

White paper

Newspapers

White T-shirt in polyester-cotton blend

Draw colorful pictures on white paper. Images will be reversed on shirt; be sure lettering is written in reverse. Pad ironing board with newspaper and cover with sheets of white paper. Place shirt on ironing board, inserting several sheets of white paper between front and back. Carefully brush away all crayon specks from drawings, so unwanted spots don't show up on shirt. Lay pictures(s) face down on shirt. Set iron to cotton setting and press down on picture. Do not move iron back and forth, or picture may blur. Image is transferred when it's slightly visible through back of paper.

Note: Shirt may be machine washed in cold water. Air fluff, then line dry.

Finger-Paint Paper

Large sheet of finger-painting paper
Finger paint
10 × 12-inch shirt box
2 sheets white or colored tissue paper
Curling ribbon

Wet sheet of finger-painting paper. Let kids decorate wet paper with finger paint. Suggest they scribble in *"Happy Mother's Day"* with their fingers. When paper dries, place shirt in box lined with tissue. Fold tissue back over shirt and close lid. Wrap box in paper and tie with several lengths of curling ribbon held together. Curl ends of ribbon with scissors.

Toffee Bars in "Not Another Tie!" Box

MAKES 32 BARS; 2 OR 3 GIFTS

I can remember one Father's Day when everyone gave Grandad a tie. After about the third package, he joked, "If someone's put a tie in this box, I'm going to hang them with it!" If the men in your life have more ties than they know what to do with, this toffee in a box makes a welcome and amusing alternative.

"Not Another Tie!" Box
(Instructions for one box)

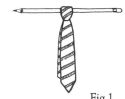

1 necktie box at least 1-inch deep

1/4 yard striped or solid oxford-cloth fabric

Fabric glue

1 necktie

Hot glue gun

4 or 5 shirt buttons

Brass brad or tie tack

Clear cellophane

1 package of toffee
(or Dad's favorite candy)

Fig.1

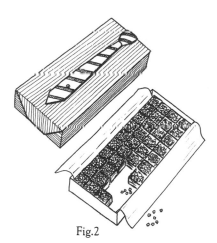

Fig.2

Prepare box lid as described in "Covered Boxes" (see Box Basics), using oxford-cloth fabric and fabric glue. If using striped fabric, line it up on box lid. Bottom of box is left uncovered.

131

Starting from narrow end of tie, measure 24 inches and cut. Tie a classic necktie knot, so that pointed end of tie is on top. Use a pencil to hold neck position in place, then adjust so there isn't a neck loop (Fig. 1). Don't pull too tight or you'll untie the knot. Top of tie should extend slightly over back of tie, or glue the tip together.

Use a hot glue gun to anchor tie on box, centered, with knot at one end. Below tie glue on 4 or 5 shirt buttons. If desired, use a brass brad or real tie tack to anchor top of tie in place. Make a small hole and push brad or tie tack through tie and lid (Fig. 2). Or, top of tie can simply be glued to bottom piece.

To assemble gift cut a piece of cellophane the length and twice the width of box. Center cellophane in box bottom, extending flaps over the sides. Arrange toffee in box and fold flaps back over bars, to protect back of lid.

If you want to indulge Dad's taste buds, use this home-made toffee recipe.

Toffee

1 1/2 cups all-purpose flour

1/4 teaspoon salt

3/4 cup firmly packed light brown sugar

1/2 cup (1 stick) butter or margarine

1/4 cup maple syrup

6-ounce package butterscotch chips

2 Tablespoons butter

1 Tablespoon water

2 cups chopped walnuts

Preheat oven to 375°F (190°C).

Combine flour, salt, sugar, and 1/2 cup butter in mixing bowl and blend until crumbly. Pat into bottom of 9 × 13 baking pan, lined with parchment paper. Bake 12 minutes.

Meanwhile, melt maple syrup, butterscotch chips, 2 tablespoons butter, and water in top of double boiler over simmering water. Blend until mixture is smooth. Stir in nuts. Spoon topping over warm crust. Spread evenly over crust to within 3/4-inch of edges. Return to oven and bake for 10 minutes. Cool completely and cut into 1-inch squares.

Jumping Jack-O-Lanterns

MAKES 1 GIFT

My dog Panda steals balls from our neighbor's tennis court, especially the orange ones. One Halloween I noticed a stash of them in his dog bed and felt it was time I returned what he'd borrowed. I decorated the orange balls with jack-o-lantern faces and wrapped them in a "Great Pumpkin" bag. The recipient was delighted and I'd hit upon a novel Halloween gift. Jumping jack-o-lanterns are perfect for tennis players and any child (or dog) who loves to play ball.

*Black felt-tip laundry marker
or black paint pen*

6 orange tennis balls

Use laundry market to decorate balls with classic jack-o-lantern faces. Some inks may bleed a little on fuzzy surfaces.

Great Pumpkin Bag

Orange paper gift sack

X-Acto knife

2 sheets black tissue paper

*2 yards each orange and
black curling ribbon*

Cut out jack-o-lantern face in gift bag, using X-Acto knife. (You may want to slip a piece of cardboard inside bag while working to prevent cutting into folded sides.) Line bag with black tissue and fill with balls. Cut ribbon into 12-inch lengths. Hold 6 pieces of ribbon together and tie around top of bag. Tissue should be showing through face and at top edge. Curl all streamers with scissors.

134

Opposite: Spring Chickens, *page 124*
Eggsquisite Easter Tree, *page 126*

Trick-or-Treat Halloween Wreath

MAKES 1 GIFT

Hanging up a Halloween wreath is like having a welcome mat for little witches and goblins, letting the neighbors know a house is truly in "spirit" with the trick-or-treat tradition. Children love to help assemble, and disassemble, this decoration.

Rolls orange and black curling ribbon
(9 yards each)

14-inch straw wreath

12 8-inch squares of white tissue paper

12 foil-wrapped chocolate Kisses™

12 9-inch squares white cotton fabric

Black felt-tip laundry markers

Assorted Halloween candies:
miniature Baby Ruth™ and Butterfinger Bars™,
Tootsie Rolls™, packages of M&M's™
or Reese's Pieces™.

Hold ends of orange and black ribbon together. Tie ribbon securely around wreath in 1-inch intervals. Keep orange and black ribbon spread apart while you wrap, so one color doesn't cover the other. When wreath is wrapped, anchor ribbon to original knot.

Cut five 1-yard lengths of both orange and black ribbon. Hold ribbons together and tie around wreath at point where wrapping begins and ends, covering with a wide layer of ribbon. Tie ribbon in knot and curl all 20 streamers. Cut twelve 10-inch pieces of black ribbon.

Opposite: "Super Mom" Custom T-Shirt, page 129
Toffee Bars in "Not Another Tie" Box, page 131

Wad up a tissue around each chocolate kiss. Place wad in center of cotton square. Gather cotton around wad and tie a ribbon in a knot under wad to create a ghost. Use laundry market to draw eyes and mouth on ghost. Attach ghost to ribbon on wreath. Slip ribbon streamers underneath strands of wrap. Repeat to make 12 ghosts. Evenly space ghosts in circle.

Fill in around wreath, by tying candy to ribbon wrapping. Cut 10-inch pieces of orange ribbon and anchor candies to wreath, tying a knot in middle of each candy. Curl all ribbon ends on ghosts and candies with scissors.

Halloween Wrap

2 sheets black tissue paper
2 sheets orange tissue paper
Orange and black curling ribbon

Place wreath in center of double thickness of black tissue paper. Cover wreath with 2 sheets orange tissue paper. Gather paper together at both long ends, enclosing wreath at sides. Tie ends with small pieces of ribbon. Cut four 15-inch lengths of ribbon in each color, for each end. Divide colors in half, equally. Hold ribbons together and tie around ends. Curl all streamers with scissors.

Pumpkin Popcorn Balls

MAKES 12 BALLS

Popcorn balls make a perfect parent-child project. You boil the syrup and your child molds the popcorn into pumpkins. For Halloween, use candy corn for Jack-O-Lantern faces; for Thanksgiving, use plain pumpkins. These also make a nice Halloween party favor or table setting treat for "Turkey Day" dinner.

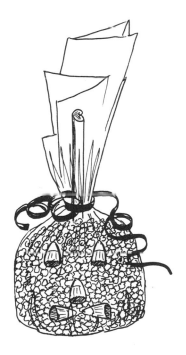

8 cups popped popcorn

1 1/2 cups sugar

1/2 cup light corn syrup

1/2 cup water

1 teaspoon white vinegar

1/2 teaspoon salt

2 teaspoons grated orange peel

*3/4 cup (1 1/2 sticks) butter
or margarine, softened*

1 teaspoon vanilla extract

1/2 teaspoon orange extract

Orange gel food coloring

Chocolate candy corn

12 cinnamon sticks

Place popcorn in very large bowl. Combine sugar, corn syrup, water, vinegar, salt, and orange peel in 2-quart saucepan. Heat to boiling over medium heat, stirring constantly to 260°F on a candy thermometer, or until small amount of mixture dropped into ice water forms a hard ball.

137

Remove from heat and stir in butter, vanilla and orange extracts. Stir in enough orange food coloring to make syrup bright orange (color will fade somewhat when added to white popcorn). Pour syrup in thin stream over popcorn, and gently stir with buttered wooden spoon.

When cool enough to touch, but still warm, shape into 4-inch balls with buttered hands. Press candy corn into balls to resemble Jack-O-Lantern faces. Push cinnamon stick halfway into top of each ball for pumpkin stem. Place on waxed paper or foil to cool. To speed hardening, refrigerate for about 20 minutes.

Pumpkin Wrap

12 twelve-inch squares orange or
clear cellophane (food approved)

Orange and black curling ribbon
(or use orange and brown for Thanksgiving)

Place each pumpkin in center of cellophane square. Cut twelve 12-inch lengths ribbon from each roll. Bring sides of cellophane up around pumpkin stem and tie an orange and black ribbon held together around cellophane at base of stem. Curl ribbon streamers with scissors.

Maple-Leaf Cookies

MAKES 36 TO 48 COOKIES; 4 GIFT BAGS

Similar to gingerbread with a mellow maple flavor, these cookies make a lovely Thanksgiving gift. Use a leaf-shaped cutter, or a real maple leaf for a pattern. Kids love cutting these cookies out and collecting autumn leaves for the bags.

1 cup (2 sticks) butter or margarine, softened

2/3 cup firmly packed dark brown sugar

1/2 cup maple-flavored syrup

1/3 cup milk

3 1/2 cups all-purpose flour

1/4 teaspoon ground ginger

1/4 teaspoon nutmeg

Preheat oven to 375°F (190°C)

Combine butter, sugar, and syrup in a medium saucepan. Bring to boil, stirring until butter melts. Remove from heat and stir in milk. Cool to room temperature. Combine flour, ginger, and nutmeg in bowl; blend in syrup mixture to make smooth dough.

Divide dough in half and wrap each portion in plastic wrap. Chill at least 2 hours. Working with one half a a time, roll out dough 1/4-inch thick on lightly floured surface. Cut with leaf-shaped cutter. Place cookies on cookie sheet lined with parchment paper. Score veins on leaves with knife. Bake 6 to 8 minutes, or until bottoms are nicely browned. Remove and cool on wire racks.

Maple-Leaf Bags

8 clear cellophane bags
Maple leaves
4 yards each brown, yellow,
and orange curling ribbon

Slip one cellophane bag into another for double-layer bags. Slip leaves between bags in attractive arrangement. Fill each bag with 9 to 12 cookies. Cut ribbon into 1-yard lengths. For each bag hold 3 colors of ribbon together and tie on top. Curl streamers with scissors.

Note: Gather maple leaves and press between sheets of waxed paper for several weeks, or until firm; or use fresh leaves.

Hanukkah Cutout Cookies

MAKES 60 COOKIES; 2 GIFTS

Cutting sugar cookies from Star of David and dreidel patterns is a festive activity for children. They enjoy decorating gift boxes as well as the cookies.

1 ¼ cups powdered sugar

1 cup (2 sticks) butter or margarine, softened

1 teaspoon vanilla extract

½ teaspoon almond extract

1 egg

2 ½ cups all-purpose flour

1 teaspoon baking soda

1 teaspoon cream of tartar

White Frosting

(recipe follows)

Tube of blue decorator's frosting

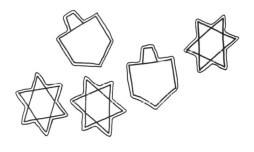

Preheat oven to 375°F (190°C).

Cream sugar and butter until light and fluffy. Add vanilla and almond extracts and egg; blend well. Combine dry ingredients, then mix into batter. Cover bowl with plastic wrap. Chill at least 1 hour. Trace Star of David and dreidel patterns onto cardboard (or use cookie cutters).

Star of David Pattern

Divide dough into 3 parts. Work with one part. Keep remainder refrigerated. Roll dough out on floured board to ⅛-inch thickness.

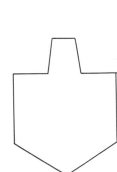

Driedel Pattern

Cut around patterns or use cutters. Place cookies 1 inch apart on cookie sheet lined with parchment paper. Bake 6 to 9 minutes or until edges are golden. Repeat with remaining dough. Cool completely and remove from paper. Spread frosting on cookies, smoothly covering to edges. Allow frosting to set. Outline cookies in blue.

White Frosting

1 1/2 cups powdered sugar

1/4 teaspoon almond extract

3 to 4 Tablespoons milk

Blend sugar, almond extract, and just enough milk to make spreadable opaque glaze.

Shining-Star Boxes

2 nine × three-inch glossy white gift boxes
or bakery-style pie boxes

Blue glitter paint or glue in writing tube

2 yards blue cellophane or Mylar tissue

2 yards metallic blue curling ribbon

Decorate tops and sides of boxes using glitter paint to make Stars of David. Dry thoroughly. Cut cellophane in half, and line each box. Arrange about 30 cookies in each box. Fold edges of cellophane back over cookies. Close lids. Cut ribbon in half and tie around each box, catching corners. Curl ribbon streamers.

Crispy Christmas Trees

MAKES 12 TREES

Children love to help mold marshmallows and rice cereal into Christmas trees with cinnamon-stick stems. These can be wrapped in cellophane and hung from a treal tree. Children enjoy making these edible ornaments as gifts for their friends.

¼ cup (½ stick) butter or margarine

10-ounce package miniature marshmallows

3 to 4 drops green food coloring

6 cups crisp rice cereal

12 cinnamon sticks

Red cinnamon candies

Melt butter in 2-quart saucepan over medium heat. Add marshmallows and food coloring, stirring until smooth and completely melted. Remove from heat; stir in cereal, coating evenly. With wet fingers mold into 12 cone shapes on foil-lined tray. Push cinnamon sticks in base of cones to resemble tree trunks. Decorate trees with cinnamon candies. Chill until firm. Remove from foil.

Hanging Wrap

12 15-inch squares green or clear cellophane

Green or red curling ribbon

Place each tree, diagonally, in center of cellophane square. The end of tree trunk should be exactly in the center. Fold bottom corner up into a triangle, so point meets the opposite point above the tree (Fig. 1). Cut twelve 12-inch lengths of ribbon. Fold each one into a loop, and knot halfway (Fig. 2). Bring all cellophane corners together at the same point. Tie with ends of ribbon loop, and curl ends (Fig. 3).

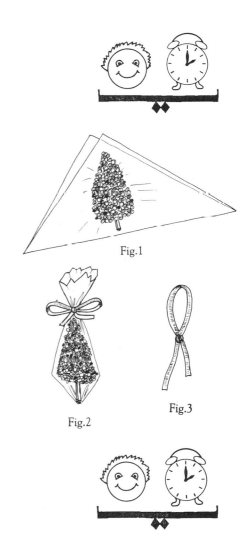

Fig.1

Fig.2

Fig.3

◆◆◆

Nutcracker Christmas Wreath

MAKES 1 GIFT WREATH

Unshelled nuts are sold in bulk at bargain prices during the Christmas season. 'Tis the season to crack your own. It's part of the tradition. Opening a bag or can of honey-roasted nuts would ruin the ritual. The beauty of this gift is that you're giving both a distinctive door decoration and nuts for snacking.

Hot glue gun

Assorted nuts:
unshelled walnuts, unshelled almonds,
unshelled pecans, unshelled filberts,
or unshelled hazelnuts

12 to 14-inch grapevine wreath

⅔ yard 2-inch wired red or green plaid ribbon

2- to 3-inch toy soldier ornament

Use hot glue gun to glue nuts all over top and sides of wreath. Do not glue nuts to back. Try to arrange nuts in an attractive random fashion. Save enough to fill gift box. Tie ribbon around wreath, through center. Tie into bow, catching loop or hook of soldier ornament in bow.

Nest of Nuts

14 × 14 × 5-inch or 16 × 16 × 5-inch
white cake or gift box

2 sheets each, red or green tissue paper

Reserved nuts from wreath project

2 yards ¾- to 1-inch wide red
or green plaid ribbon

Metal nutcracker or nut pick

Line box with doubled sheets of tissue paper. Cross sheets in middle of box, allowing excess to hang over sides. Place wreath in box. Fill center and corners with reserved nuts. Fold edges of tissue back around wreath and close lid. Tie ribbon around box, catching opposite corners. Tie nutcracker or pick into bow.

◆◆◆

Store-Bought Cookie Creations

So you say you can't bake? No problem. With a little melted chocolate and some supermarket cookies, you can create spectacular centerpieces. Kids will love to get their hands into this project. In fact, these chocolate chip cookie concoctions are featured in *The Children's Party Handbook* as part of a "Cookie Factory" party. You can use your imagination and substitute almost any type of cookie.

Colossal Cookie Tree

8 dozen chocolate chip cookies
7-inch plastic plate or cake board
Chocolate Glaze (recipe follows)
Pecan Pinecones (recipe follows)
3 dozen red and green candied cherries

Dip bottoms of cookies into chocolate glaze and all over surface of plate. Repeat dipping and stacking cookies in layers, gradually tapering into a tree shape. Use melted chocolate to attach red and green cherry ornaments and pecan pinecones. Drizzle any remaining chocolate in thin stream over sides of tree. Allow several hours for chocolate to completely set.

Chocolate Chip Cookie Wreath

About 1 cup of Chocolate Glaze
(recipe follows)
2 dozen chocolate chip cookies
9- or 10-inch plastic plate or cake board

1 dozen Pecan Pinecones
(recipe follows)
12 each red and green candied cherries, halved

Spread chocolate glaze on backs of 8 cookies. Arrange in circle on plate. Repeat process, overlapping with second row of 8 cookies. Top off with final row of 8 cookies, overlapping second row. Drizzle wreath with remaining chocolate. Decorate with cherries and pecan pinecones. Allow about 2 hours for chocolate to set.

Chocolate Glaze: Melt together two 12-ounce bags of semisweet chocolate chips, 2/3 cup butter-flavored vegetable shortening, and 1/3 cup white corn syrup in double boiler over simmering water. This makes enough for tree, wreath, and pinecones.

Pecan Pinecones: To make pinecones use about 1 cup of pecans and 1 cup of melted chocolate. Place one pecan on sheet of waxed paper. Dip two pecans in chocolate and overlap first pecan. Then overlap with three, then overlap with two again. There will be 8 pecans in each pinecone. Allow to harden on waxed paper.

Pecan Pine Cone (close-up)

Red-Cellophane Wrap

For Tree: Use 3 yards cellophane, cut into two 1 1/2-yard pieces. Crisscross sheets on table, with tree in center. Bring sides up around tree, securing at top in tassel. Tie with 12 inches of 1-inch wide red plain ribbon. Trim cellophane edges with pinking shears.

For Wreath: Simply place wreath off center on 1-yard sheet of cellophane. Bring long side over top of wreath, meeting edge of short side. Gather cellophane into tassel at side of wreath. Tie with 12 inches × 2-inch wide wired red plain ribbon. Trim edges of cellophane with pinking shears.

◆◆◆

Holiday Dressed-Up Doughnuts

1 TREE, 12 WREATHS, 12 SNOWMEN

Doughnuts go stale soon after you buy them. However, when doughnuts become hard as a rock they make wonderful holiday decorations. (You can even buy dozens of day-old doughnuts, or doughnut holes, at a discount.) Wrap these in cellophane and ribbons as gifts for friends and neighbors.

Doughnut Hole Tree

10-inch Styrofoam cone
Royal Icing (page 197)
Green gel food coloring
2 to 4 dozen doughnut holes
(amount varies depending upon size)
2 dozen pecan halves
8 red candied cherries (split in half)
8 green candied cherries (split in half)
Pastry bag with leaf tip

Prepare royal icing and tint it green with food coloring. Spread layer of icing on cone and cover with doughnut holes. Fill pastry bag with icing and pipe leaves in the spaces between doughnuts. Decorate with pecans (to resemble pinecones) and cherries (to resemble tree ornaments). Allow frosting to dry overnight (Fig. 1).

Fig.1

148

Cellophane Wrap

2 yards green cellophane

4 yards each of red and green curling ribbon

Pinking shears

Cut cellophane into a pair of 1-yard sheets. Cut ribbon into 1-yard lengths. Overlap sheets of cellophane, criss-crossing each other. Place tree in center and bring edges of cellophane up around the sides, gathering in a tassel. Hold ribbons together and tie around the base of tassel in a secure knot. Curl streamer of ribbon with scissors. Trim top of tassel with pinking shears.

Doughnut Wreath Ornaments

12 glazed yeast doughnuts (very dry)

Royal Icing (page 197)

Green gel food coloring

4-ounce container of candied citron
(red and green)

Silver dragées

Pastry bag with leaf tip

Donut Wreath

Prepare royal icing and tint green. Fill pastry bag with icing and pipe around doughnuts (in an overlapping fashion) to resemble leaves. Cut citron into tiny pieces (about 1/4-inch cubes). Use citron and silver dragées to decorate wreaths. Allow to dry overnight.

Fig.2

Cellophane Wrap

10 yards 14-inch red satin ribbon

4 yards clear cellophane

Cut ribbon into a dozen 24-inch lengths and a dozen 6-inch lengths. Cut cellophane into twelve-inch lengths. For each wreath: Bring a 24-inch piece of ribbon through the center doughnut and tie around doughnut. Hold ends of ribbon together and tie in a knot. Wrap doughnut in cellophane, gathering around the ribbon loop. Take 6-inch piece of ribbon and tie around gathered cellophane (Fig. 2).

Doughnut Snowmen

12 cake doughnuts coated
in powdered sugar (very dry)

24 cake doughnut holes coated
in powdered sugar (very dry)

Royal Icing (page 197)

Chocolate brown gel food coloring

12 toothpicks

1 yard of 1/4-inch red satin ribbon,
cut in 3-inch lengths

12 red, foil-wrapped chocolate Kiss™ candies
(remove paper tabs)

Pastry bag fitted with star tip

Pastry bag fitted with round writing tip

Fig. 3

Fig.4

Opposite: Trick or Treat Wreath, page 135

Tint about 1/2 cup of icing brown and set aside in a small covered container. Fill pastry bag (with star tip) with white icing. For each snowman: Fill the center of a full-size doughnut with some frosting. Place a doughnut hole on top. Insert a toothpick in the center of doughnut hole. Wind a piece of 3-inch ribbon around toothpick, like a scarf (Fig. 3) and hold in place with about a teaspoon of icing. Stick another doughnut hole on top of toothpick. Pipe a swirl of white icing on top of doughnut hole and place a candy on top. (This will look like a red Santa hat with fur trim.) Pipe a star on top of hat for a pom-pom effect. Fill pastry bag (with writing tip) with brown icing. Pipe dots on snowman for eyes, nose, mouth, and buttons. Allow to dry overnight (Fig. 4).

Rainbow Wrap

6 sheets (20 inches × 30 inches) rainbow Mylar tissue
12 yards rainbow curling ribbon

Cut sheets of Mylar tissue in half (20 inch × 15 inch sheets). Cut ribbon into 12-inch lengths. For each snowman: Place each figure in the center of a Mylar tissue sheet. Bring sides up around snowman and gather in tassel at top. Hold 3 pieces of ribbon together and tie in a knot around the base of tassel. Curl ends of streamers with scissors.

Note: Doughnut decorations will last for a month or two when thoroughly dried. Obviously, these are not meant to be eaten!

Opposite: Pumpkin Popcorn Balls, page 137

Almost Edible Architecture

MAKES 6 TO 8 "COTTAGE" GIFTS; 1 "PALACE" GIFT

Gingerbread houses are synonymous with the holidays. However, they can be a hassle, even for experienced bakers. My first spot on the "Today Show" featured an array of edible architecture from a cuckoo clock to Noah's Ark. I struggled for weeks to make one barn. As a joke, Tom Brokaw broke off the roof, minutes before air time. I've since learned to take such projects lightly—as they should be. Sure, these are made with edible items, but who really wants to dismantle and consume a stale cookie house? I'll settle for the security and simplicity of a cardboard frame.

Cream Carton Cottages

2 batches Royal Icing
(recipe follows)

6 pints or 8 half-pint cream or milk cartons

Pretzel sticks or rods the length of cream cartons

12 to 16 large shredded wheat biscuits

6 to 8 one-and-one-half-ounce milk chocolate bars

3 to 4 dozen 1-inch classically shaped pretzels

Red cinnamon candies

Prepare royal icing. Keep portion you're not immediately using in covered container. Spread evenly around the sides of cream cartons. Line cartons with horizontal rows of pretzel rods to resemble log cabins.

Carefully split shredded wheat biscuits in half with sharp knife. Trim tab on top of cartons down to about ³⁄₈-inch and tape shut. Spread frosting on each side of lid, and press on each side, one slice cut-side down, to resemble thatched roof. Cut chocolate bars into 2- and 3-piece segments. Use 2-piece segments for windows and 3 piece segments for doors. Attach chocolate to cottages with dabs of icing. Use 1-inch pretzels for shutters around the windows.

Tint remaining icing green and spoon into a pastry bag fitted with a small-leaf tip. Pipe garlands of evergreen around windows and doors, etc. Press red candies onto green icing.

Allow houses to dry 24 to 48 hours, depending upon humidity.

Rainbow Wrap

These make exquisite place markers or party favors for a holiday meal. Wrap each cottage in 20 × 30-inch sheet of rainbow Mylar tissue, with a tassel at top. Tie with strips of 1-inch wide plaid ribbon.

Pink Sugarplum Palace

3 batches Royal Icing

Empty, clean half-gallon milk carton

Tape

2 empty 16-ounce round oatmeal cartons

Aluminum foil

3 to 4 pounds pink jelly beans or peppermint candies

2 three-and-one-half-ounce milk chocolate Toblerone™ bars

2 dozen Hershey's Chocolate Kisses™

2 one-and-one-half-ounce milk chocolate bars

Two, 3 1/2 to 4-inch candy canes

Chocolate-covered Cones
(recipe follows)
10 × 24-inch piece of heavy cardboard covered with pink or red foil
Green colored sugar
1 dozen spearmint leaf gumdrop candies

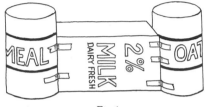

Fig.1

Fig.2

Prepare 2 batches royal icing and keep in covered container. Prepare milk carton by cutting down to about 7-inch height. Use trimmed carton and tape to make flat top. Place carton on its side and tape oatmeal cartons to each end (Fig. 1). Tint royal icing pink.

Place cardboard structure on foil and cover entire surface with icing. Working quickly, place jelly beans as if you were laying stones in "cement." When surface of structures is completely covered, use icing to attach Toblerone bars across the top edges of milk carton. Attach 12 equally spaced Chocolate Kisses around tops of each oatmeal carton.

Prepare chocolate-covered cones for towers. Anchor 3 towers in center of castle with icing. Cut chocolate bar so you have one large "drawbridge" and several single segments for small windows. Use pink icing to attach drawbridge in front of castle, with candy canes along sides. Attach small windows to the front and back sides with icing (Fig. 2).

Allow structure to dry 24 to 48 hours, depending upon humidity. When icing is very hard, carefully lift structure from foil, peeling it away from base. Prepare one batch royal icing. Spread on foil-covered cardboard, to within 1 inch of edge. Sprinkle green sugar over icing. Mount castle on cardboard, pressing into icing, and "landscape" with gumdrop leaves for bushes. Allow to dry another 24 hours.

Drop-Cloth Drape

Cut a medium weight, clear plastic painter's drop cloth into a 2 1/2 yard square. Place palace in the center and bring sides up around it. Gather into a tassel at top and tie with multi-streamers of pink and green curling ribbon.

Royal Icing

3 egg whites

1 pound powdered sugar

Beat egg whites and powdered sugar on high speed with electric mixer, until stiff peaks form. Because this dries fast, work quickly and keep any unused portion in a covered plastic container. (It helps to make this in single batches.)

Chocolate-Covered Cones

1 three-ounce block paraffin wax

6 ounce bag of semisweet chocolate chips

3 sugar ice cream cones

3 paper flags on toothpicks

Melt paraffin in small, narrow saucepan. Add chocolate and stir until smooth. Hold cones over saucepan and dip into chocolate, allowing excess to drip back in pan. Set cones, upside down on foil-lined tray. When chocolate is firm to touch, insert flags through small holes in tops of towers.

◆◆◆

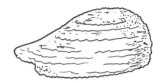

Fig.1

Fig.2

New Year's Buffet "Boar's" Head

MAKES 16 SERVINGS

When I was in school, my favorite festivity was Revel's Day. The students dressed in Old English costumes and sang Christmas carols. We perched the smallest preschool child on top of a yule log and pulled it into the dining hall. Then the upperclassmen carried in "the boar's head." (It was really a plaster artifact from the prop department of drama class.)

As an adult, I wanted to recapture this tradition for New Year's dinner. However, I'm no hunter. So, I created a facsimile using ground ham. This simple recipe is more like a sculpture than a meatloaf. It's a work of art that will truly entertain friends. It's also a lot easier to carve than the real thing.

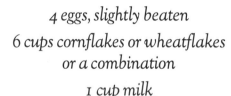

4 eggs, slightly beaten

6 cups cornflakes or wheatflakes
or a combination

1 cup milk

1/2 cup frozen apple-juice concentrate, thawed

1 Tablespoon Worcestershire sauce

1 Tablespoon onion powder

2 teaspoons celery salt

1 teaspoon garlic powder

1 teaspoon thyme

¼ teaspoon ground clove

3 pounds ground ham or turkey ham

3 pounds ground pork or veal

Aluminum foil

2 long, curved, knobby carrots for boar's tusks

2 jumbo pimiento-stuffed olives

1 spiced or pickled crab apple with stem

1 baking potato

Preheat oven to 375°F (190°C).

Combine eggs, cereal, milk, apple-juice concentrate, and seasonings in very large mixing bowl. Mix until ingredients are well-blended. Mix in ground meats. Line large roasting pan with foil. Shape meat mixture into boar's-head form with a snout (Fig. 1).

Push carrots into sides of cheeks to resemble "tusks." Push apple under snout, so it looks as if it's in the boar's mouth. Insert olives in head for eyes. Split potato in half lengthwise. Hollow out centers, leaving potato shells. Insert one on each side of head for ears (Fig. 2). Bake 1½ to 1¾ hours.

If excessive fat accumulates in pan, draw it off with a bulb baster and discard. If carrots and potatoes brown too much, cover lightly with foil during last half of baking. Cool boar's head slightly, then use large metal spatulas to gently transfer it to serving platter.

$^{1}/_{2}$ *cup currant jelly*

Fresh parsley

2 yards gold foil

Safari Sauce

(See House Dressings and Custom Condiments)

Heat currant jelly in small saucepan over low heat until melted. Brush all over boar's head to glaze. To present, garnish head with parsley. If you're taking this to another house, cover with a tent of foil and bring along Safari Sauce or Quick Pineapple-Pepper Relish. And don't forget to sing "The Boar's Head Carol"! (Or another appropriate song.)

◆◆◆

MILESTONE MOMENTS

Mailbox Muffins

First Set of Wheels

Graduation Cap Candy Box

Quarter-of-a-Century Mirror

Gold "Leafed" Frame

Cake and Ice Cream Cones for the Class

Dieter's "Birthday Cake"

◆

Milestone Moments

A birthday, graduation, anniversary, or retirement all mark milestone moments in life. Even getting a driver's license, or moving into a new home is a memorable event. These rites of passage deserve to be recognized with a personalized gift. In many cases that gift could be a creative cake. Children delight in celebrating their birthday by sharing "ice cream cone cakes" with classmates. For the dieter, there's a birthday cake box with a low-calorie gift. Imagine a lovely tray of miniature wedding cakes for an anniversary party. Or, how about a "quarter-of-a-century-mirror"?

Mailbox Muffins

MAKES 2 DOZEN MUFFINS; 1 GIFT

Whether it's the very first house or the relocation to a new community, moving in is one of life's milestone moments. What makes a welcome gift? How about a new mailbox with the new address, stuffed full of savory homemade muffins! Bake a batch of confetti-pepper muffins and a batch of broccoli-basil muffins.

Basic Batter

1 egg

1 ¼ cups milk

¼ cup (½ stick) butter
or margarine, melted

2 cups all-purpose flour

1 Tablespoon baking powder

½ teaspoon salt

Confetti-pepper muffins
(recipe follows)

Broccoli-basil muffins
(recipe follows)

Preheat oven to 400°F (200°C).

Beat egg in large mixing bowl. Blend in milk and butter. Combine flour, baking powder, and salt in separate bowl. Add dry ingredients to egg mixture, along with cheese and vegetables. Stir just until moistened. Spoon batter into 12 greased muffin cups. Bake 17 to 20 minutes. Cool slightly, remove from pans.

Confetti-Pepper Muffins

1 egg

1 1/4 cups milk

1/4 cup (1/2 stick) butter
or margarine, melted

2 cups all-purpose flour

1 Tablespoon baking powder

1/2 teaspoon salt

1/2 cup grated sharp cheddar cheese

1/4 cup chopped green bell pepper

1/4 cup chopped red bell pepper

1/4 cup chopped scallions (with green tops)

Preheat oven to 400°F (200°C).

Beat egg in large mixing bowl. Blend in milk and butter.
Combine flour, baking powder, and salt in a separate bowl. Add
dry ingredients to egg mixture, along with cheese and vegetables.
Stir just until moistened. Spoon batter into 12 greased muffin cups.
Bake 15 to 20 minutes. Cool slightly, remove from pans.

Broccoli-Basil Muffins

1 egg

1 1/4 cups milk

1/4 cup (1/2 stick) butter
or margarine, melted

2 cups all-purpose flour

1 Tablespoon baking powder

1/2 teaspoon salt

1/3 cup grated Swiss cheese

2 Tablespoons grated Parmesan cheese

1/2 cup finely chopped, fresh broccoli

1/4 cup chopped fresh basil leaves

1 clove crushed garlic

Preheat oven to 400°F (200°C).

Beat egg in large mixing bowl. Blend in milk and butter.
Combine flour, baking powder, and salt in a separate bowl. Add
dry ingredients to egg mixture along with cheese and vegetables.
Stir just until moistened. Spoon batter into 12 greased muffin cups.
Bake 15 to 20 minutes. Cool slightly, remove from pans.

Personalized Mailbox

1 classic style mailbox in metal or white
Watercolor marker
Acrylic paint in color to complement house
or shutters and trim
Paintbrush
2 half-gallon plastic storage bags
with twist tops
1 yard calico or gingham fabric

Write address and name on mailbox with watercolor marker.

Use acrylic paint and brush to carefully paint over lines made with marker. Dry.

Pack each type of muffin in plastic storage bag and tie with a twist. Trim edges of plastic tassels with pinking shears. Cut fabric into one 30-inch square and three 2 × 14-inch strips. Tie fabric strips around bags covering twists in bow. Line mailbox with cloth square and fill with muffin bags. Close mailbox front and use remaining strip of fabric to tie bow around flag of mailbox.

First Set of Wheels

MAKES 1 GIFT

Passing your driving test and earning your license—this is the teenage "rite of passage." Naturally, most teens seem to expect their own car to come with the license. This humorous gift helps bring them back down to earth, while celebrating their achievement.

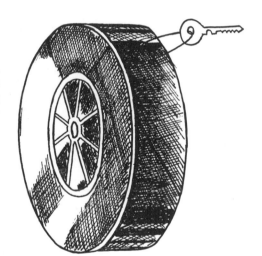

14- to 16-inch hat box
about 4 to 5 inches deep
1 yard 60-inch wide black felt
Fabric glue
Craft brush
Tailor's chalk
Silver-glitter fabric paint
Paintbrush
Scissors

Using bottom of hat box and lid for patterns, trace 2 circles on felt. Cut out. Cut strip of felt the width and circumference of box. Coat box with fabric glue using craft brush. Cover with felt. Smooth out lumps or creases. Draw a 7- to 8-inch circle in center of lid with chalk. Draw lines radiating from center, to resemble wire-wheel hubcap. Paint rim of hubcap and spokes with silver paint using paintbrush. Dry.

Opposite: Almost Edible Architecture—Cream Carton Cottage, page 152

Key to First Set of Wheels

20 × 30-inch sheet of silver Mylar tissue

20 × 30-inch sheet of wax paper

2 to 3 dozen chocolate-covered, chocolate doughnuts

*3 × 5-inch unruled index card, cut in shape
of a large key*

Black felt-tip marking pen

1 1/2 yards 1 1/4-inch thick black satin ribbon

Key to family car or dummy key

Line box with sheet of Mylar tissue and food approved wax paper (to protect doughnuts) and fill with doughnuts. Fold excess tissue back over doughnuts and cover with lid. On card using marker, write: "Key to Your First Set of Wheels." Punch hole in corner of card. Tie ribbon around box, knotting it at upper edge. String card and key onto ribbon, then tie in bow.

◆◆◆

*Opposite: Pink Sugarplum Palace, page 153
          Nut Cracker Christmas Wreath, page 144*

Graduation Cap Candy Box

MAKES 1 GIFT

While searching for unique packaging concepts, I came across a graduation cap candy box in a small gift shop. It was an inspired idea that anyone could make from an empty Brie box. For college graduates, cover the box with black or white satin; choose school colors for high school caps.

Empty 8-inch Brie cheese box

Tacky fabric glue

Craft brush

About 5/8 yard satin ribbon the width of the depth of box lid, color matched to satin

10-inch square heavy mat board

14-inch square black, white, or color-of-choice satin fabric

Tassel on 6- to 7-inch cord, same color as satin

Hot glue gun

Brush outer rim of upper lid of cheese box with tacky fabric glue using craft brush. Cover rim with ribbon. Brush one side of mat board with a smooth, even layer of glue.

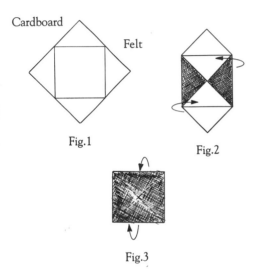

Cardboard

Felt

Fig.1

Fig.2

Fig.3

Fig.4

Fig.5

Place glued side down to wrong side of satin square. (Place board as shown in Fig. 1.) Brush exposed surface of board with glue. Fold corners of fabric onto board, with points meeting in center (Fig. 2). Smooth out lumps or creases before glue sets (Fig. 3). Dry thoroughly. Pierce small hole in top center of board with sharp, pointed object. Pull cord of tassel through hole, about $3/4$ inches.

Anchor end of cord with a dot of glue from hot glue gun. Use hot glue to fasten underside of board to top of box lid (Fig. 4). Center square on circle to resemble a graduation cap mortarboard (Fig. 5).

Bon Bon Box

2 eight-inch circles gold foil or clear cellophane

10 to 15 premium quality chocolates or truffles
(amount depends upon size and shape of candies)

Line bottom of Brie box with piece of foil and arrange chocolates in box. Top with second layer of foil and cover with mortarboard lid.

 ◆◆◆

Quarter-of-a-Century Mirror

MAKES 1 GIFT

Here's a way to commemorate the 25-year mark, be it an anniversary or birthday. The amount of coins needed depends upon the size of mirror and your budget.

Hot glue gun

Enough quarters to go around mirror 3 times

Oval or round mirror with smooth, beveled edge

Felt cut to fit cardboard

Cardboard cut to fit back of mirror

Picture wire

1/4-inch to 3/8-inch wide grosgrain ribbon, circumference of frame

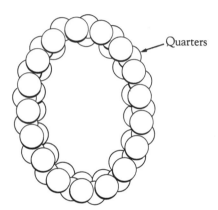

Quarters

Fig.1

Use hot glue gun to attach coins around edge of mirror once. Make second row of coins, stacking the first, just inside outside row. Make final row of coins on top of both rows (Fig. 1). Glue quarters along "seam" between both rows. To prepare backing, attach felt to cardboard with hot glue gun. Poke two holes in back of cardboard. Run wire loop through holes, allowing some slack for hanging frame (Fig. 2). The distance between holes and amount of wire will vary with size of mirror. Press wire on cardboard side very flat and glue cardboard to back of mirror. Glue ribbon around edge of mirror, covering cardboard and felt.

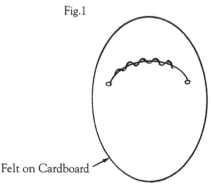

Felt on Cardboard

Fig.2

Coin Paper Wrap

Gift box slightly larger than mirror
Silver Mylar tissue
White wrapping or freezer paper
Several quarters
Silver crayon with paper removed
Silver curling ribbon

Wrap mirror in box lined with enough sheets of silver tissue to pad mirror. Add some crumpled sheets on top. Make wrapping paper by placing paper over coins and rubbing with side of crayon to rub coin design on. Wrap box with paper, taping edges to seal. Tie with 6 streamers, curling ribbon held together, catching opposite corners of box. Curl ends of streamers with scissors.

◆◆◆

Gold "Leafed" Frame

MAKES 1 GIFT

Although this is ideal for a 50th anniversary, there are many types of "golden" occasions. This gift can mark any milestone relationship that stands the test of time. It also makes a special 50th birthday present.

*10 × 12-inch wooden frame
with smooth beveled sides
Dried eucalyptus leaves
Hot glue gun
Aluminum foil
Gold spray paint
Clear urethane spray sealer*

Remove glass and backing from frame. Remove eucalyptus leaves from branches. Use hot glue gun to completely cover the surface of frame with overlapping leaves. Place back of frame on foil-covered surface. Spray frame with several light coats of gold paint. Dry between coats. Give frame a final coat of urethane sealer.

Thanks for the Memories Box

8 × 10-inch enlargement of photo of
special significance to you and recipient

10 × 12-inch white shirt box

Gold cellophane grass

1/2 × 2-inch strips white paper

Fine-tipped gold marking pen

Gold-glitter paint in writing tube

1 yard metallic gold ribbon

Reassemble frame, mounting picture inside. Line box with gold
grass and place frame on top. Write mutual memories on paper strips
with gold marking pen. Scatter papers around frame on gold grass.
Close box and write, "Thanks for the Memories!" in large glitter-
paint letters on lid. Dry lid. Tie ribbon in bow around box, catching
opposite corners.

◆◆◆

Cake and Ice Cream Cones for the Class

MAKES 30 ICE CREAM CONE CAKES

When I was a child, it was a custom to celebrate a birthday by bringing cupcakes to class. Somehow, this ritual seemed to become more important than the "at home" birthday cake. Passing out the cakes made every birthday boy and girl feel like a prince or princess of the group.

1 package any flavor cake mix

30 flat-bottomed ice cream cones

1 can chocolate frosting

1 can vanilla frosting

Red and green food coloring

Confetti candy sprinkles

30 birthday candles

Prepare cake batter according to package directions. Line cones up in 9 × 13-inch cake pan. If any cones tip, pare down any uneven seams on bottom. Pour scant 1/4 batter into each cone; cones must not be more than 1/2 full. Bake according to package direction for cupcakes. Cool completely. Open frostings and divide vanilla frosting in half. Tint one part pink and one part "pistachio" green. Frost "cones" with chocolate, pink, or green frosting. Insert candle into top of each cake.

Birthday Box

1, 14 × 14 × 5-inch white cake or gift box

Red, blue, green, pink, yellow, and orange
felt-tip markers with wide-chisel tips

Colored plastic wrap

2 yards each red, blue, green, pink, yellow,
and orange curling ribbon

Let your child write his or her age all over the box in every color
marker. Carefully arrange cones in box. Cushion cones with wadded
strips of plastic wrap to prevent any from tipping over. Hold all 5
lengths of ribbon together and tie around box, catching opposite
corners. Curl ends of streamers with scissors.

◆◆◆

Dieter's "Birthday Cake"

MAKES 1 GIFT

What do you give someone on a diet when you don't want to tempt or torment them with a fattening birthday cake? How about a beautiful birthday-cake box complete with candles. Inside you can conceal a special gift, or simply fill with air-popped popcorn for a low-calorie treat.

10 × 5-inch round hat box

About 1 yard strawberry pink moire satin fabric

About 1 yard brown 1-inch wide satin ribbon

About 3 1/2 yards strawberry pink braid

8 three-fourths-inch pink satin roses

Pink plastic candle holders
and birthday candles

Hot glue gun

Brown slick paint writing tube

Tacky fabric glue, spray mount

Cover box with moire, using method described in "The Hollywood Wrap"/Covered Cans and Hat Boxes (using fabric glue and spray mount adhesive). Around middle of box, using hot glue gun, glue a band of brown ribbon to suggest chocolate layer. Glue bands of braid around edge of bottom and lid. Glue 8 equally spaced roses around the braid on lid. Glue garlands of braid from rose to rose. Only dip down as far as first layer.

Break off stems of candle holders so that they lie flat. Hot glue to lid of box. Insert candles in holders. On top of box write in brown slick paint:

"Happy Birthday (Name)!"

This will look like chocolate icing on top of the box. Allow to dry.

Wrap a special gift in layers of pink and brown tissue paper or line box with tissue paper and fill with unbuttered, air-popped popcorn.

8

BRIDAL AND BABY SHOWER BOUNTY

Wedding Cake Keepsake Boxes

Bride's Button-Box Sewing Kit

Fabric-Bag Lamps

Smoked Chicken Salad Swans

Baby Bootee Cakes

Bassinet Baby Dolls

Rub-a-Dub Tub Baby Bath Bucket

◆

Bridal and Baby
Shower Bounty

B ridal and baby showers are a lot like the real thing—when it rains, it pours. It seems like everyone is either getting married or giving birth. Because these celebrations usually center around the same circle of friends, custom-made bridal and baby gifts are always refreshingly different.

Sometimes the best shower gifts are actually "Hostess Helpers." Smoked chicken salad swans make a lovely luncheon dish. For a baby shower, how about pink or blue bootee cakes?

Wedding Cake Keepsake Boxes

MAKES 1 GIFT

Satin-covered three-tiered hat boxes look like a wedding cake and are a clever way to package a dessert serving set. Later, the bride can use boxes to store wedding memorabilia. Use a hot glue gun to attach silk flowers or a small bridal ornament on top.

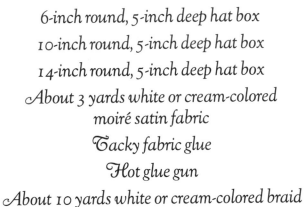

6-inch round, 5-inch deep hat box

10-inch round, 5-inch deep hat box

14-inch round, 5-inch deep hat box

About 3 yards white or cream-colored
moiré satin fabric

Tacky fabric glue

Hot glue gun

About 10 yards white or cream-colored braid

20 ½-inch satin roses (sold in fabric stores)

Wedding cake ornament or silk flowers

Glue-on Velcro™ squares

Opposite: Wedding Cake Keepsake Boxes

Cover boxes with moiré using tacky fabric glue and spray mount adhesive as described in "The Hollywood Wrap." To visualize decorations, stack boxes from largest up to smallest, like a wedding cake. Hot glue rows of braid at lid and base rims around boxes. Then glue 8 roses, equally spaced, around large box on braid around lid. Repeat with middle box. Use only 4 roses for top box.

Hot glue "garlands" of braid from rose to rose around each box. Attach ornament or flowers to lid of top box. Position Velcro tabs between layers of box lids and bases, then glue in place. This will help hold stack together with option of separating boxes.

Dessert Service Set

This is a natural packaging for a dessert service set. If someone's already giving one to the bride, you might consider teaming up on the gift. Wrap pieces in tissue and place in center-tier box. Fill top and bottom boxes with tissue and potpourri.

Opposite: Graduation Cap Candy Box, page 168
            Cake and Ice Cream Cones for the Class, page 174

Bride's Button-Box Sewing Kit

MAKES 1 GIFT

Do you keep a jar of odd-ball buttons around your house? Over the years, I've accumulated an incredible collection of spares. Buttons are a wonderful decorative resource. Why not use them to cover a Brie box? For a bride in need of basic equipment, this makes a clever sewing kit.

1 nine-inch Brie box

Aluminum foil

Spray paint in color of choice

Assorted buttons without shanks

Hot glue gun

*1 yard grosgrain ribbon width of lid rim
and color to complement*

Sewing Kit Set-Up
(list follows)

Place box lid on sheet of foil, so top is facing up. Spray with 2 coats of paint. Dry thoroughly between coats. Cover top of box with buttons, attaching with hot glue gun. Glue ribbon around the rim of box lid. Allow about 6 inches of overhang, then double end under about 3 inches, making a loop. Glue flat to box. Select one very attractive button and glue in place, 1 inch from end. Ribbon should look as if it's buttoned in place around box.

Sewing Kit Set-Up

Small pair of scissors
Small, flat, pin cushion to fit in box
Thimble
Package assorted needles
Package straight pins
Seam ripper
Snaps
Tailor's chalk
Small spools basic color thread
Neatly arrange sewing equipment in box.

Buttons and Bows Wrap

1 yard chintz fabric
Rubber band
1/2 yard each of 1/8-inch wide
grosgrain ribbon in 3 to 4 colors
to coordinate with fabric
Buttons with holes

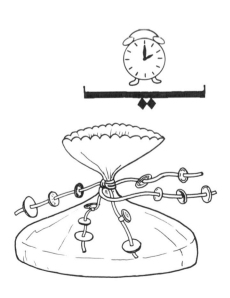

Using pinking shears, cut 36-inch circle out of fabric. Place sewing kit in center of wrong side of fabric. Gather fabric together in tassel at top. Secure in place with rubber band. Hold ribbons together and tie in tight knot, just below rubber band. Remove rubber band. Thread several buttons on each streamer, tying knots between buttons to evenly space. Tie knots at ends of streamers.

Fabric-Bag Lamps

MAKES 1 PAIR OF LAMPS; 1 GIFT

I first spotted a pair of these lamps in a pricey decorator shop, and was immediately drawn to them. But this basic, yet brilliant idea is simple and inexpensive to make. It's the perfect gift for a bride, especially if the lamp set is coordinated to the fabric in a room.

1 pair inexpensive ginger-jar lamps

*Glazed chitz fabric or designer sheet
(amount depends upon lamp size)*

Thread for sewing machine

Rubber bands

1 yard cord or ribbon to coordinate with fabric

2 forty-watt flame globes

Note: I remove the shade entirely and replace bulbs with flame globes to create "lanterns." If desired, you could use the shades by covering with fabric.

Measure lamp by running tape measure from neck, around bottom of base and back up to other side of neck. Add 10 inches to this measurement. Cut 4 circles of fabric, the diameter of this total measurement. For each lamp, pin two circles, right sides together. Sew around circle with 1/4-inch seam, allowing a 2 1/2-inch opening (Fig. 1).

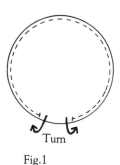

Turn

Fig. 1

Turn right sides out, and press. To make opening for cord, place lamp in center of circle and mark where side of fabric would touch base of cord. Make a machine buttonhole at this spot, large enough for plug to go through (Fig. 2). Place lamp back on circle and draw fabric up around sides of lamp, pulling cord through hole. Secure gathered fabric around neck of lamp with rubber band. Slit colored cord in half. Tie secure bow around neck of each lamp. Slip off rubber band. Knot ends of cord or ribbon for a finished look. Replace standard light bulbs with flame globes (Fig. 3).

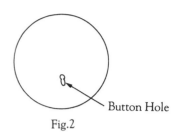

Button Hole

Fig.2

Tissue-Bag Wrap

8 sheets tissue paper in color to coordinate with fabric
Rubber bands
1 yard of same cord or ribbon used on lamps

For each lamp, lay double sheets of tissue paper, crosswise on double sheets of tissue. Place lamp in center and bring sides of tissue up around lamp. Secure gathers at top with rubber band. Cut cord in half. Tie bow around tissue. Remove rubber band. Finish ends of cord by knotting.

Note: If lamps are taller than one length of tissue allows, try taping extra doubled sheets of tissue together to form longer sheets.

Fig.3

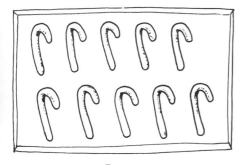

Fig.1

Smoked Chicken Salad Swans

MAKES 12 SWANS

Cream-puff swans are usually seen gracefully floating among Floating Islands on dessert carts. However, they are equally intriguing as entrees. Try stuffing swan-shaped puffs with smoked-chicken salad for a shower luncheon.

1 cup water
¹/₂ cup (1 stick) butter
1 cup all-purpose flour
4 eggs
Pastry bag with medium writing tip
Smoked-Chicken Salad
(recipe follows)

Preheat oven to 400°F (200°C).

Bring water and butter to rolling boil in large saucepan. Add flour, all at once. Reduce heat and stir vigorously until mixture forms ball, about 1 minute. Remove from heat and beat in eggs, one at a time, using wire whisk.

Line small cookie sheeet with parchment paper. Fill pastry bag with ¹/₂ cup dough. Pipe twelve, 2 ¹/₂-inch "cane" shapes onto paper (Fig. 1). Bake 20 minutes. Cool completely on wire rack. Meanwhile, drop remaining dough in 12 equal-sized mounds, 3 inches apart on ungreased cookie sheet lined with parchment. Bake 40 to 45 minutes until puffed, golden brown and dry. Cool on wire rack.

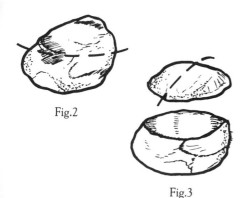

Fig.2

Fig.3

Cut off tops of puffs with sharp knife (Fig. 2). Scoop out and discard soft dough. Carefully split tops of puffs in half (Fig. 3). Fill puffs with chicken salad, inserting neck and halved tops of puffs as wings. Chill until serving time.

Note: These will become soggy, and are best assembled the day of serving.

Smoked Chicken Salad

4 cups cubed smoked chicken or turkey

1/2 cup finely chopped celery

*1/3 cup chopped watermelon pickle
or bread and butter pickles*

1/3 cup toasted chopped almonds

3/4 cup regular or nonfat mayonnnaise

2 teaspoons brown mustard

1 Tablespoon honey

1/2 teaspoon Worcestershire sauce

1/2 teaspoon salt

2 Tablespoons fresh minced chives

Fig.3

Combine chicken, celery, pickle, and almonds in a large mixing bowl. In a small bowl, blend mayonnaise with mustard, honey, Worcestershire, salt and chives. Add mayonnaise mixture to chicken mixture and toss to combine.

Note: Buy slightly more than 1 pound smoked chicken or turkey, sold unsliced, from a deli or gourmet food store.

Swan Salad-Bar Boxes

Parsley
2 large, clear plastic salad bar boxes
Green curling ribbon

Wash thoroughly, dry and chill parsley several hours. Chop enough to yield 4 cups. Line each box with 2 cups parsley. Arrange 6 swans in each box. Close lids and tie shut by wrapping each box with 8 lengths of ribbon held together. Tie ribbons together in knot on top of box. Curl all 16 streamers on each box.

Baby Bootee Cakes

MAKES 20 CAKES

This baby-shower classic is made by cutting cupcakes into the shape of little shoes. Baby bootees may be pink or blue, cherry or blueberry. Not sure of the baby's sex? Bake a batch of both or use lemon cake mix for yellow bootees.

1 box (18.5-ounce) white cake mix,
prepared as directed with egg whites, oil and water

1/2 cup chopped maraschino cherries
or fresh blueberries

30 cupcake liners

3 (16 ounce) cans of vanilla buttercream frosting

Red or blue gel food coloring

Small pastry bag with round writing tip

Preheat oven to 350°F (175°C).

Prepare cake mix, folding cherries or blueberries into batter. Line 30 muffin tins with paper liners and spoon batter into cups about half full. Bake 20 to 25 minutes, or until a toothpick inserted in center comes out clean.

Cool completely. Remove paper liners from cakes. Cut 10 cakes in half as shown (Fig. 1). Cut the other 20 cakes, slicing off 1/4, as shown (Fig. 2). Use the 3/4 cupcake as the "heel." Place half cake, cut-side down next to cut-part of heel for "toes," as shown (Fig. 3), on sheet of waxed paper. Reserve 1/4 cup frosting and tint remainder either pink or blue. Frost bootees.

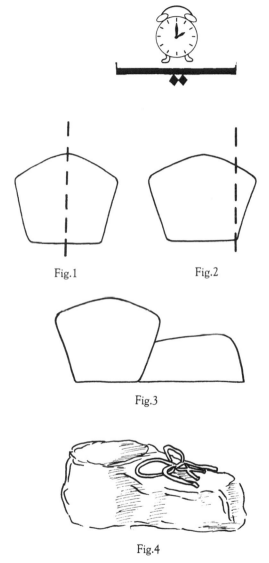

Fig.1   Fig.2

Fig.3

Fig.4

Fill pastry bag with reserved white frosting and pipe laces on bootees (Fig. 4). Place cakes in freezer for a few minutes to set frosting.

Note: It may be necessary to bake cakes in batches to make all 30.

Bootee Box

Pink or blue acrylic paint
Metal pie plate
Pair of old bootees
10 × 15 × 3½-inch white cake box
20 four-inch white paper doilies
Pink or blue curling ribbon
Pair of new bootees

Pour paint in pie plate, and use soles of bootees for printing little "footprints" walking all over box. Dry. If box is flat, fold tabs and assemble. Use a metal spatula to lift semifrozen cakes off waxed paper and onto doilies. Arrange cakes in box and cover. Cut off four, 2-yard lengths curling ribbon. Hold ribbons together and tie around box, catching corners at opposite ends. Tie laces of new bootees together and tie into ribbon streamers. Curl all 8 streamers.

Note: For yellow bootees, simply use lemon cake mix. Substitute lemon extract for almond in frosting, and tint with yellow food coloring. Use yellow paint and ribbon on box.

Bassinet Baby Dolls

MAKES 1 GIFT

Cute, cushy little stuffed socks are strung together for hanging across the crib. Use all white or assorted colors of infant socks with decorative borders around ankles.

2 yards ¼-inch wide satin ribbon in color
to coordinate with ankle borders of socks

3 pairs of infant socks

Fiberfill

Embroidery yarn in color to match ball fringe

Thread to match socks

Piece of ball fringe with 5 balls, in color
to complement ribbon

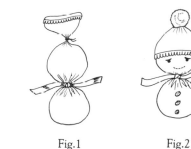

Fig.1   Fig.2

Cut off five, 6-inch pieces of ribbon. Stuff 5 socks with fiberfill, filling to cuff. Tie each ribbon in a knot tightly around center of sock. Tie the top closed with embroidery yarn (Fig. 1). Fold cuff down over "head," folding edge back up about ½ inch for cuff of stocking cap. Slip-stitch around stocking-cap cuff, securing it to the head. Sew ball of fringe to top of stocking cap. Sew on eyes and mouth of fabric with embroidery yarn. (Fig. 2).

Fig.3

Select a doll for center of string. If using pairs of socks in 3 different colors, this should be the one without a mate. Tie remaining ribbon around neck of doll, so that it crosses over ribbon in front and knots at back of neck. Doll will be in center with 21 inches of ribbon on each side.

Take strands of short ribbon at neck front and tie by slipping one end under second neck band and catching into the knot of a bow. Tie remaining socks onto string, about 6 inches apart. Take ends of ribbon and tie knots with 1-inch loops (Fig. 3) for hanging from crib.

Crib Pillowcase Package

Double sheet white or pastel tissue paper
Crib-size pillowcase
12-inch piece of ¼-inch wide satin ribbon
Reserved infant sock from bassinet babies

Place string of bassinet babies along lengthwise edge of tissue paper. Roll up in tube. Wind tube into circle and stuff into pillowcase. Stand pillowcase up. Tie ribbon around open end, forming 3- to 4-inch top knot. Make bow with ribbon ends, tying sock into the knot.

Note: When hanging anything over a crib, be sure it's securely fastened and well out of your baby's reach.

Crib Pillow Case Package

Rub-a-Dub Tub Baby Bath Bucket

MAKES 1 BATH BUCKET GIFT

Among gift services, baskets full of baby things are the hottest-selling item. It's no wonder. New parents can't seem to get enough basic baby equipment. A customized bath bucket will make a most welcome gift.

White, yellow, and orange fabric paint

Metal pie plate

Natural sponge

Light blue plastic utility pail or bucket

Light blue or white baby T-shirt

Paintbrush

Black laundry marker

Duck-shaped sponge

Paring knife

2 bars of mild white or yellow soap
about 2 × 3 inches

2 nine-inch squares yellow tulle fabric

12 inches 1/4-inch wide light blue satin ribbon

Pour white paint into pie plate. Pat natural sponge into paint and print puffy clouds around the top of pail. Pour yellow paint into dish. Continue to decorate pail and T-shirt by pressing duck sponge into yellow paint. Print ducks all over sides of pail and on front of shirt.

Dry. Use paint and brush for adding whites of eyes and orange beaks on ducks. Dry. Dot pupils of eyes with laundry marker. Use paring knife to make simple soap sculpture. Carve each bar of soap into duck shape. Gather piece of tulle around each bar of soap. Cut ribbon in half and tie tulle in tassel. Trim edges with pinking shears.

Note: Precut printing sponges are sold in most craft stores. You can make your own by drawing a pattern on a 3/4-inch thick kitchen sponge and cutting out with scissors, using duck pattern. With either commercial or homemade sponge, always premoisten and squeeze dry before printing.

Baby-Bath Supplies

Baby shampoo

Baby powder

Baby oil

Pale yellow and blue wash cloths

Rubber duck

Toy boat

Bath sponge
(may be trimmed to duck shape)

Arrange all supplies in bucket, along with baby shirt, neatly folded or rolled, and hand-carved soaps.

9

GREETINGS, GOODBYE, AND GET WELL GIFTS

"Come-for-Coffee" Cappuccino Cookies

Potpourri Pet

Seashell Sachets in Fishnets

Life's a Bowl of Cherries

Sunday Comics, Coffee, and Croissant Tray

Quick-Fix Goodbye Gifts

◆

Greetings, Goodbye, and Get Well Gifts

Saying hello seems warmer when creativity comes with the introduction. Imagine welcoming a new neighbor with come-for-coffee cups filled with cappuccino cookies. Saying goodbye is a lot harder, and a custom-made gift eloquently expresses your sentiments.

Get-well gifts are often the most appreciated of all. When someone is ill, a thoughtful gesture really gives them a lift. Unfortunately, few of us give get-well gifts much thought. But imagine the delight of waking up to a breakfast tray covered with a favorite Sunday comic strip. Children of all ages will enjoy a colorful popcorn-ball bush or lollipop topiary tree. And what about good old-fashioned chicken soup? Grandma's cure for the common cold and flu can be delivered with "happy-face" balloons for a fast recovery.

"Come-for-Coffee"
Cappuccino Cookies

MAKES 2 DOZEN COOKIES; 4 GIFT MUGS

This is an original way to greet a new neighbor. Cappuccino cookies in coffee mugs are an open invitation to meet for a midmorning chat.

½ cup (1 stick) butter or margarine, softened

½ cup firmly packed dark brown sugar

*1 Tablespoon instant cappuccino,
dissolved in 2 Tablespoons hot water*

¼ teaspoon cinnamon

¼ teaspoon grated orange peel

⅛ teaspoon salt

1 ½ cup all-purpose flour

¼ cup toasted, chopped pecans

Preheat oven to 350°F (175°C).

Cream butter and brown sugar together. Blend in cappuccino, cinnamon, orange peel, and salt. Mix in flour and nuts to form a dough. Mold into 1-inch balls and place on cookie sheet lined with parchment paper. Bake 12 to 14 minutes, just until cookies are set. Cool completely and remove from paper.

"Come-for-Coffee" Mugs

*4 generic looking coffee mugs
in white or cream color*

Brown ceramic paint

Narrow paintbrush

Clear or rainbow cellophane

1 yard brown satin ribbon

Using paintbrush paint "Come For Coffee" on mugs with ceramic paint. Dry overnight. Fill each mug with 6 cookies. Cut cellophane into 1/2-yard sheets. Cut ribbon into four 9-inch lengths. Place mug in center of each sheet of cellophane. Bring edges up around mug and tie at top using ribbon. Tie ribbon in bow, and trim cellophane tassel with pinking shears.

Potpourri Pet

MAKES 1 GIFT STATUE

This all-purpose gift is appropriate for so many occasions. It's easily made by coating an inexpensive ceramic animal statue with glue and potpourri. To personalize the gift, find out the recipient's favorite animal: a dog, cat, or teddy bear.

Aluminum foil

*4 to 5 cups potpourri
(buy commercial prepared or
see section on Potpourri Pointers)*

*Ceramic animal statue or bank
(10 inches or less)*

Tacky craft glue

Craft brush

Scented potpourri spray

12 to 18 inches 1/4-inch wide velvet ribbon

Small locket or dog tag (optional)

Spread out several sheets of aluminum foil to cover work surface. Crush potpourri with rolling pin. Coat statue heavily with glue using craft brush. Roll statue in potpourri. Pat potpourri into patches where it didn't stick; dry. Fill in any gaps with extra glue and pat on handfuls of potpourri.

Mist statue with scented potpourri spray; dry. Tie ribbon in knot around animal's neck. Thread locket or tag onto ribbon streamer. Tie into bow.

Tissue and Nosegay Wrap

6 to 8 sheets tissue paper in assorted or single color
Rubber band
16-inch piece of $\frac{1}{2}$-inch wide velvet ribbon
in same color used for statue
4-inch paper doily
Cluster of dried flowers with stems
trimmed to 5 inches

Gently wrap potpourri pet in 2 to 4 layers of tissue paper. Spread 2 sheets tissue paper on table. Cover with 2 more sheets of tissue, crisscrossing. Place wrapped statue in center. Bring tissue up around sides, gathering in a tassel at top. Secure in place with rubber band. Tie ribbon under rubber band in knot. Remove rubber band. Wrap doily around flowers "cornucopia-style." Tie into ribbon with bow. Trim tissue-paper tassel with pinking shears. Spread paper to form pom-pom.

Seashell Sachets in Fishnets

MAKES 4 SACHET SHELLS; 1 GIFT

When you're meeting someone for the first time, a sachet is always a safe gift to give. Everyone appreciates the personal touch, and a sachet is so simple to make.

*4 scallop or oyster "au gratin" shells
(available in cookware stores)*

*4 ten-inch squares of shell pink
or peach tulle fabric*

*2 cups potpourri (use commercially prepared
or homemade; see "Potpourri Pointers")*

Rubber bands

*2 feet each of $\frac{1}{8}$-inch wide shell pink
or peach and seafoam green satin ribbon*

*4 one-quarter-inch stitch-on shell pink
or peach satin roses*

Shell pink or peach thread

Place one shell on each square of tulle slightly off center. Fill each shell with 1/2 cup of potpourri. Gather tulle around each shell in tassel. Gather tulle at the base of scallop shell, or at one edge of oyster shell. Secure in place with rubber band. Cut ribbon into 6-inch lengths. Holding green and pink ribbons together, tie knot around tulle, just under rubber bands. Remove rubber band. Tie ribbon streamers in bows. In center of each bow, stitch a rose over the knot in shell pink thread.

Wicker-Plate Wrap

1 sheet seafoam green tissue paper

9-inch wicker paper plate holder

*30-inch square shell pink or
coral tulle fabric*

Rubber band

*3 feet each $1/8$-inch wide shell pink or
coral and seafoam green satin ribbon*

Fold up tissue and cut into thin shreads with pinking shears. Line plate holder with nest of shredded tissue. Arrange sachet shells in tissue. Place plate holder in center of tulle. Gather edges of tulle around plate, and into tassel on top. Secure tulle with rubber band. Cut ribbon into 12-inch lengths. Hold all streamers together, and tie in knot around tassel just underneath rubber band. Tie ribbon in bow. Remove rubber band. Trim edges of tassel with pinking shears.

Life's a Bowl of Cherries (Chocolate-Covered)

MAKES 40 CHERRIES; 1 GIFT

This get-well gift is also appropriate for sweetening those bittersweet moments, such as moving away, retiring, or leaving a job.

2 ten-ounce jars maraschino cherries with stems

$1/4$ cup ($1/2$ stick) unsalted butter, softened

1 Tablespoon cherry-flavored liqueur

1 Tablespoon light corn syrup

2 cups powdered sugar

2 twelve-ounce bags of semisweet chocolate chips

3 Tablespoons butter-flavored shortening

Drain cherries. Dry on paper towels overnight. Cream butter with liqueur and corn syrup. Blend in sugar and knead until smooth to make fondant. Form a scant teaspoon of fondant around each cherry. Place on foil-lined cookie sheet. Chill for one hour.

Melt chocolate with shortening in top of double boiler over simmering water. Hold cherries by stem and dip in chocolate. Allow excess chocolate to drip back into dipping pot before setting on foil. If a second coating of chocolate is necessary, chill cherries for 30 minutes before redipping. Chill cherries after final dip until chocolate is set.

"Life's a Bowl of Cherries"
(Chocolate-covered)

Cherry Bowl

1 ½ quart white or cream ceramic bowl
Cherry-red ceramic paint
Paintbrush
1 yard red net or tulle fabric
Rubber band
8-inch piece of ¼-inch wide red satin ribbon

On ceramic bowl using ceramic paint and brush, write on side of bowl, freehand style:

"Life's a bowl of cherries!"
(chocolate covered)

Dry thoroughly. Gently pile cherries into bowl. Place in center of net fabric. Bring edges of fabric up around bowl and gather in tassel at top. Secure in place with rubber band. Tie ribbon in bow just underneath rubber band. Remove rubber band. Trim edges of net with pinking shears.

Sunday Comics, Coffee, and Croissant Tray

MAKES 1 GIFT

This breakfast tray is bound to perk up anyone who is recuperating in the hospital or at home. It can be made from an assortment of comic strips, or collected clippings of the patient's favorite funny-paper character.

*Clippings of color comic strips
(enough to cover top and
bottom of tray twice)*

1 plain plastic service tray

Decoupage polymer, gloss type

Paintbrush

When covering tray, reserve your favorite comic strips for second layer on top side of tray. To begin, coat bottom side of tray with layer of polymer using paintbrush. Arrange comic strips on tray so edges overlap and tray doesn't show through. Smooth out bubbles and wrinkles. Dry thoroughly. Turn over and repeat process on top side. When top is dry, turn over and repeat on bottom again. When bottom is dry, turn over and cover with final layer of comic strips.

Give each side 3 coats of polymer. Allow each coat to dry thoroughly before applying another.

Breakfast in Bed

Fresh brewed cup of coffee

Glass of orange juice

2 croissants on colored paper plate

Miniature jars of preserves or marmalade

Comic section of newspaper

*6-inch strip of 2-inch wide satin ribbon
in bright color*

Colored plastic knife

Bright-colored napkin to match plate

Arrange coffee, juice, croissants, and preserves on tray. Roll up newspaper and tie ribbon around it, in bow. Place knife on plate and tuck under edge of plate. Place newspaper on tray and present to patient before coffee gets cold.

This is also a great gift for children. Substitute hot cocoa for coffee.

◆◆◆

Quick-Fix Goodbye Gifts

Gifts that you give for the last time, last in memory. If you're short on time, here are some thoughtful ways to say farewell.

Bon Voyage Bag: If someone's just going off to school or on a long trip, he or she can always use travel supplies. Fill a clear plastic cosmetic bag with sample-size, personal care products and toiletries. Include some snacks, film, and a good novel. Wrap the whole thing up in a map of the destination.

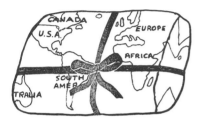

Bon Voyage Bag

Remember to Write Set: We always say "keep in touch," but how soon we forget. One way to remind a friend is to make it easier. Start by wrapping up a stationery set with pre-addressed, stamped envelopes to you. On the wrapping paper, stamp FIRST CLASS, all over the package.

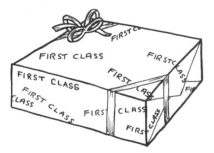

Remember to Write Set

Goodbye Box: In a way this is a treasure chest of mutual memories. It also makes a good group gift. Collect old photos of times shared with a friend, along with mementos of special events. Include favorite things like a preferred cologne or perfume or a favorite candy or snack food. Throw in any item you've ever borrowed and forgotten to return. Wrap everything up in an attractive hat box, then have all the contributors sign goodbye with felt-tip markers all over the box.

Goodbye Box

10

WAYS WITH WRAPS

Newspaper Wrap

Other Nontraditional Wrapping Papers

Custom-printed Papers

Crisp Corners for Classic-shaped Boxes

Papers for Unconstructed Wraps

Fabric Wraps

Wrapping Cylinders and Tubes

The Hollywood Wrap

Bags

Ribbons and Bows

Box Toppers

◆

Ways with Wraps

When you need wrapping paper don't immediately buy a roll from your local card and party shop. There are unique wrapping supplies at home just waiting to be discovered. You may not have to look any further than the morning paper. Newspapers are great for wrapping specialized gifts because there is an appropriate section for almost every type of gift or personality.

Newspaper Wrap

Comic Pages: for birthday gifts, children's gifts, or get-well gifts

Sports Section: sporting-goods equipment or any gift for a sports fan

Fashion Page: ideal for wrapping women's apparel

Cooking Section: for cookbooks and kitchenware

Real Estate/Home Section: for home-decorative pieces, such as doormats, lamps, and pillows

Wedding Announcements: a good wrap for shower and wedding gifts, especially if you can get the page with the actual bride and groom

Travel Section: an interesting way to wrap souvenirs purchased during a trip or vacation

Business Section or Wall Street Journal: a great executive gift wrap

Classified Car Ads: this section is a fun way to wrap gifts for car buffs and teenage boys

When using newspaper wrap, newsprint can be messy, coming off on fingers and on the gift. A solution to this problem came about during the Victorian era. The butler ironed the newspaper so the lady or gentleman of the house would not soil their robes in the morning.

As decadent as this may sound, it's an excellent idea. The heat sets the ink on the paper. Dry iron newspaper pages at a medium setting before using them as a gift wrap. Despite the humbleness of newsprint, don't be afraid to use elaborate ribbons and bows. The contrast can be quite effective.

Opposite: Baby Bootie Cakes, page 191
Bassinet Baby Dolls, page 193

Other Nontraditional Wrapping Papers

Wallpaper

Posters

Maps

Childrens' Art and Finger Paintings

Sheet Music:
ideal for wrapping records,
CD's, and tapes

Opposite: *Ways With Wraps, page 211*

Custom-Printed Papers

Brown parcel-wrapping paper and white freezer paper are inexpensive and ideal for custom printing. Freezer paper can be used on either the matte or shiny side. Here are some ideas for custom prints:

Rubber Stamps: Rubber stamp with either your name or initials, or the recipient's, can be purchased from stationery stores. Use colored ink pads to stamp random rows all over the paper.

Stencils: Stencils and stencil paint are available at craft stores. You can make your own stencils by using an X-Acto knife to cut designs from sheets of plastic acetate. Lightly apply paint to paper, patting onto surface using a dry, blunt-end stencil brush. Press the stencil on the paper and the paint is "pounced" over stencil. (Pouncing means putting paint through a stencil with the flat tipped end of a stencil brush.)

Sponge Printing: Both cellulose and natural sponges are wonderful tools for creating interesting effects on paper. By dipping square or rectangular edges of sponge into paint, you can print in rows to resemble a checkerboard or a wall of bricks. Natural sponges make beautiful marble-like designs. You can use one or several colors of acrylic paint.

I like to use layers of pastels such as lavender, pink, and pistachio green, allowing paint to dry between colors. Precut sponges can also be purchased in all sorts of shapes such as animals, flowers, or stars. You can also cut your own from a flat household sponge.

Doily Painting: Gold or silver spray paint and paper doilies create beautiful snowflake-like designs. Simply lay doilies on top of paper and lightly spray the surface. Carefully lift doilies before paint dries. Doilies can be reused until you've sprayed an entire roll of paper.

Spatter Painting: Flicking wet paint from a brush onto paper can create attractive abstract designs. Try using several complementary colors together.

Vegetable and Potato Prints: This process can produce elegant prints. Lemons, oranges, potatoes, onions, and peppers work best when sliced in half and allowed to dry overnight. Potato halves can be carved into shapes or letters (a good way to print initials). Whole corn cobs make interesting impressions and celery tops can be used as a paintbrush. Press dry vegetables into acrylic colors or metallic paints and stamp-print all over paper.

Crayon Rubbings: Leaves, coins, wood bark, and rough-textured surfaces make interesting patterns when rubbed onto paper. Place paper over objects and gently rub back and forth with the flat side of a bare crayon.

Free-Hand Designs: One of the easiest ways to create custom paper is to use felt-tip markers. Draw designs, pictures, and patterns, or simply write one long running message, over and over again. An effective wrap for a group gift is to have everyone autograph the paper.

Crisp Corners for Classic-Shaped Boxes

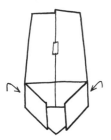

Square and rectangular boxes are simple to wrap. But sloppy corners can ruin the presentation. To avoid this, start with the right size sheet of paper. Here's my rule of thumb:

Width = 2 times box height plus length plus 1 or 2 inches

Length = 2 times box height plus 3 times box width minus 2 inches

Place box upside down in center of paper. Bring sides up tightly around box and tape in a seam down the middle. For average to narrow widths, neatly fold corners as shown (Fig. 1) and tape (Fig. 2). For wide boxes, especially square ones, fold corners in at sides (Fig. 3) and tape at ends (Fig. 4).

When paper isn't large enough, piece together with double-stick tape so the seam is at the bottom of the box that becomes the top. Always conceal this type of top seam with a wide band of ribbon. When wrapping a fragile box that can't be flipped over, wrap from underneath and conceal the top seam with ribbon.

◆◆◆

Fig.1

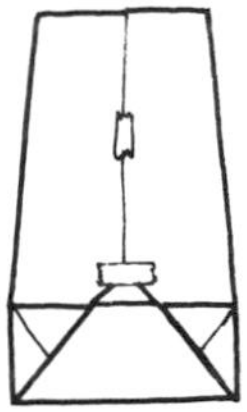

Fig.2

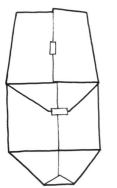

Fig.3

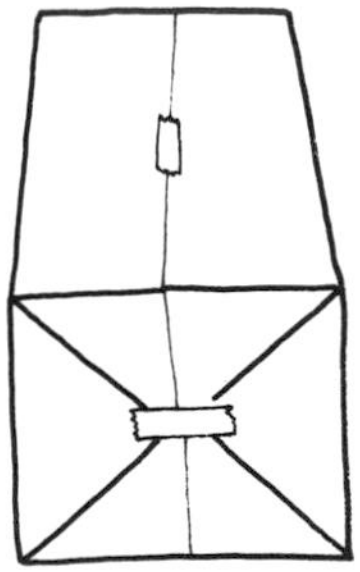

Fig.4

Papers for Unconstructed Wraps

We all know how frustrating it is to wrap bulky, odd-shaped objects. In fact many of the projects in this book easily fit that description. Tissue paper, Mylar tissue, cellophane, and even trash bags were made to meet such challenges. Mylar tissue is a modern miracle. It comes in beautiful gold, silver, and colored metallics. My personal favorite is the rainbow Mylar tissue. This pearl-like transparent tissue reflects the colors of a prism. It's an exquisite wrap for cookies, candies, and foodstuffs. (But be sure always to wrap food in wraps labeled "food approved.")

Throughout this book, I refer to a basic method of unconstructed wrapping. I place the object in the center of one sheet of wrap (Fig. 1) or two sheets, crisscrossed (Fig 2). The amount of wrap needed will be determined by the width of the wrap and the size of the object. I bring the edges of the wrap up around the object and gather into what I refer to as a tassel on top (Fig. 3). It helps to secure this tassel, temporarily, with a rubber band. For a pom-pom effect, the top is trimmed with pinking shears. A ribbon is tied tightly, just underneath the rubber band, which is removed (Fig. 4).

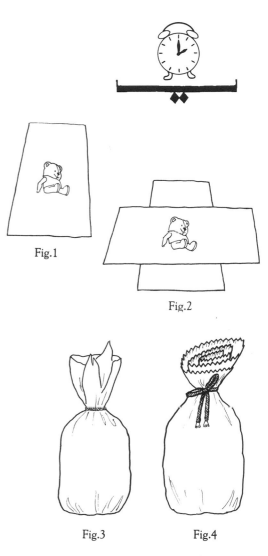

Fig.1

Fig.2

Fig.3　　　　Fig.4

Fabric Wraps

The Japanese are the ultimate gift givers and gift wrapping experts. They recognize fabric as a fabulous material for wraps. The "furoshiki," as it is called in Japan, is a square piece of fabric used to tie around boxes. Quite often, the luxurious silks or linens for furoshiki would make impressive gifts. You can adapt the concept using anything from humble gingham to gossamer tulle.

Fig.1

For a furoshiki wrap, place a box upside down, on the wrong side of cloth, at a right angle to the diagonal. Bring lower corner of fabric over top of box. Roll the box over so that it's right side up, wrapping the cloth around as you go (Fig. 1). Bring upper corner over box (Fig. 2). Bring ends up around box (Fig. 3) and tie in a knot (Fig. 4).

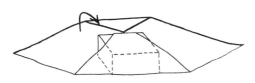

Fig.2

Of course, any fabric can be wrapped around an object using the same method described in "Papers for Unconstructed Wraps" using tissue paper, Mylar tissue, or cellophane.

When it comes to decorating fabric, use fabric paints. These are more flexible than acrylic paints and many will hold up to machine washing.

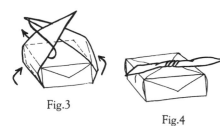

Fig.3

Fig.4

Choose shiny slick paints, glitter paints, glow-in-the-dark paints, or, my favorite, puff paints. Puff paints do exactly that; once dry, the paint is ironed and it puffs up in relief. This is ideal for decorating children's gifts with fuzzy animal designs. Most fabric paints come in easy-to-use writing tubes. You can also adapt many of the printing methods described in "Custom Printed Papers" on fabric.

A beautiful fabric wrap is like giving a gift with a gift. In fact, how about giving a scarf as the gift wrap, furoshiki-style.

Wrapping Cylinders and Tubes

Cylinders and tubes can be wrapped with crisp paper or soft wraps such as tissue, Mylar tissue, cellophane, or fabric. Crisp edges call for pleating the paper. Soft edges can be tied in a tassel giving a firecracker effect.

To wrap a cylinder, you'll need to have the circumference of the gift plus 2 inches for width. Length varies. For crisp edges, you need only allow for length plus diameter. The overhang at each end will be one half the diameter. Soft edges need an overhang on each end of at least 3 times the diameter. That means you'll need a sheet of paper that's at least the length of the gift plus 6 times its diameter.

Pleated Edge: After wrapping the cylinder and securing with tape (Fig. 1), neatly tuck in corners with a series of pie-shaped pleats (Fig. 2). Secure in place with tape or a decorative sticker (Fig. 3). A bow is often used to conceal the top, if cylinder is standing upright (Fig. 4).

Soft Edge: Gather edges together with ribbon or cord at each end. Edges may be pinked (Fig. 5) or shredded with vertical cuts for a firecracker effect (Fig. 6).

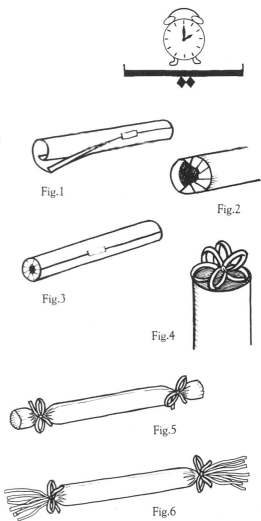

Fig.1

Fig.2

Fig.3

Fig.4

Fig.5

Fig.6

Paper Tubes

The charming English custom of Christmas crackers is an idea that can be applied to year-round gift wrapping. Christmas crackers are small tubes of cardboard containing candy or trinkets. The tubes are rolled in paper and tied at the ends with ribbon (Fig. 1). These also are attractive when wrapped with soft tissue or Mylar tissue and multistreamers of curling ribbon. For wedding favors, wrap tubes in satin moire fabric and tie with lace (Fig. 2).

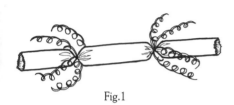

For tubes, you can simply cut paper-towel or wrapping-paper tubes into desired lengths. Tubes are also the perfect protective container for wrapping rolled-up posters and prints.

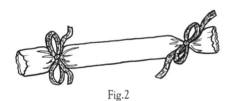

Fig.1

Gift Tins

A gift tin or can is the only container that keeps certain types of baked goods fresh. Tins keep moisture in or out depending upon the desired effect. There are many beautifully decorated tins available. When buying tins, I usually shop for smart-looking solid colors such as red, silver, or gold.

Fig.2

I also recycle used fruitcake cans. If you're like me, you probably received scores of them over the years. Don't throw out the can. Even if the tin has a company design or print, it can be covered with paint. Use a base metal primer, then two coats of metal paint. Separate lid and base, placing openings down on a drop cloth. Spray outside surface only. For the most attractive presentations, line tins with cellophane or Mylar tissue (but only let the food come in contact with wraps labeled "food approved.")

Jar Lids

Jar lids are simple to cover. You can have professional results rivaling those of gourmet products. Some crisp papers work well. However, flexible Mylar tissue and fabrics are ideal for this purpose. Jar lids can be covered with circles cut about 3 inches larger than the diameter of the lid (Fig. 1), or with squares measuring twice the diameter (Fig. 2).

The simplest way to secure the wrap around the neck of the jar is with elastic cord. This can be precut, tied, and slipped over the top of the lid. If using a ribbon, secure the wrap in place with a rubber band first. Tightly tie the ribbon around the jar, just underneath the rubber band. Then remove the rubber band.

Wine-Bottle Wraps

Bottles of wine, liqueur, Champagne, and sparkling water make wonderful gifts; always welcome and a logical present to bring when you're a dinner guest.

The gift-wrapping industry recognized this by offering wine-bottle sacks. But don't settle for an off-the-rack sack. Decorate it with any of the methods described in "Custom-Printed Papers."

For example: My favorite wrap for a bottle of Grand Marnier is a gold sack printed all over with a slice of dried orange dipped in orange paint (Fig. 3).

Another quick way to wrap a bottle is again borrowed from the Japanese furoshiki concept. It's simple and very striking. Place the bottle in the center of a large 30-inch square of fabric. Bring the two opposite corners of fabric together (Fig. 4). Tie corners on top and cross remaining corners in front of bottle (Fig. 5). Wrap corners around bottle (Fig. 6) and tie on other side (Fig. 7).

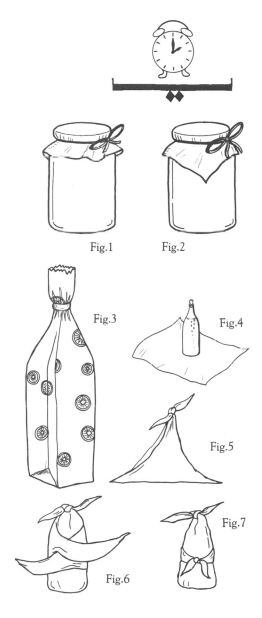

Fig.1 Fig.2

Fig.3 Fig.4

Fig.5

Fig.6 Fig.7

Here's a cute way to dress-up a bottle with a shirt and tie. Simply cut off an old shirt sleeve and sew up the bottom. Slip the bottle into the sleeve so that the cuff comes up around the neck like a collar (Fig. 8). Cut a necktie in half and use the smaller half to make a baby-size tie. Tie around the neck of the bottle, and fold down cuff edge, like a collar (Fig. 9).

Fig.8   Fig.9

The Hollywood Wrap

I grew up watching old movies and TV shows where no one ever struggled with wrapping paper. Gifts always arrived in perfectly wrapped two-piece boxes. The actress would pull off the lid and inside was a mink coat. Only in Hollywood would anyone receive a package wrapped like that, complete with the mink coat! This lack of realism always frustrated, but also fascinated, me.

When high-quality coverings such as fabrics and wallpapers are used, a two-piece box is a beautiful gift. Just look at the rebirth of hat boxes as room accessories.

Any box suitable for the Hollywood wrap should be made of fairly sturdy cardboard. A two-piece square or rectangular box must have rigid sides.

Commercially-made hat boxes are available in many gift shops. However, these are often wrapped with thin, inexpensive paper. If the paper is securely glued and smooth, the box can be successfully recovered with high-quality fabric or wallpaper. (The fabric should be opaque, so the original pattern does not show through.) Many tins can also be covered in a similar style.

Square or Rectangular Boxes

Wallpaper or fabric
Drop cloth or large sheets of foil
Wallpaper paste or spray mount adhesive
Square or rectangular box with lid
Tacky craft or fabric glue

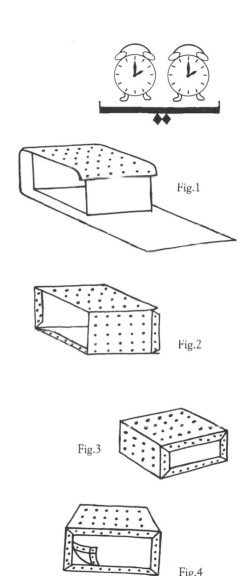

Fig.1

Fig.2

Fig.3

Fig.4

Cut paper or fabric to measurements of box:

Side band: A strip of paper or fabric that goes around all sides of box, adding 2 inches for the seam. Width of sideband should be the height of the box, adding 3 inches for seams.

Box bottom: This piece of fabric or paper should be 1 inch shorter than the length of the box, and 1 inch narrower than the width of the box. When centered on the bottom, the box will extend 1/2 inch around all sides.

Box lid: This piece of fabric or paper should be 2 inches longer and 2 inches wider than the measurements of the top.

Place paper or fabric wrong side up on a clean work surface covered with drop cloth. Coat paper with wallpaper paste or spray fabric with adhesive. Start wrapping around box, as shown, 1 inch past the corner edge. Keep box centered so that there's a 1$1/2$-inch overhang at each edge (Fig. 1). Smooth out lumps and wrinkles while you work. When you're almost to the starting edge, fold back a 1-inch hem, then glue down, using tacky craft glue, so there's a smooth seam on the edge. On open edges of box, make a 1/2-inch hem on the overhang, fold down edges and glue around the inside rim of box (Fig. 2). Slash overhang in corners at the box bottom, and fold corners diagonally. Glue down hem around bottom of box (Fig. 3). Glue on bottom sheet (Fig. 4).

For Lid Box: Coat wrong side of paper or fabric with paste or spray. Center the box lid in the middle. Smooth sides up around lid (Fig. 5), fold and miter corners as if wrapping a gift box (Fig. 6). Using tacky craft glue, glue all sides up against box, then turn under hem and glue around inside of lid (Fig. 7).

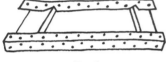

Fig.5

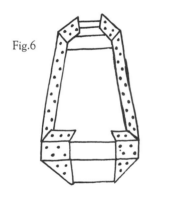

Fig.6

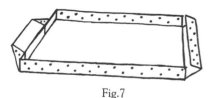

Fig.7

Hat Boxes and Covered Cans

Hat box
Wallpaper or fabric
Drop cloth or large sheet of foil
Wallpaper paste or spray mount adhesive
Tacky craft or fabric glue

Cut paper or fabric to measurements of box:

Lid top: A circle to fit top of lid.

Lid sideband: A strip that will go around the box lid, allowing an additional 2 inches for the overlapping side seam. Width of strip should be 3 inches wider than the lid band.

Box bottom: A circle the exact measurements of the box bottom.

Box sideband: A piece long enough to go around the box, allowing an additional 2 inches for the overlapping side seam. Width should be the depth of the box, allowing an additional 3 inches for foldover around rim and at base.

First cover sidebands of box and lid, using the method for covering square or rectangular box (Fig. 1). There should be a $1^1/_2$-inch overhang around the opening and base (or top) of box (or lid). Make $^1/_2$-inch hem in the overhang around opening, then glue down to the inside rim of box. Cut slashes in the overhang around base (or box lid) (Fig. 2). Glue down tabs (Fig. 3). Glue top and base circles over tabs (Fig. 4). If desired, glue a braid around raw edges of fabric circle on lid and at the base of box (Fig. 5).

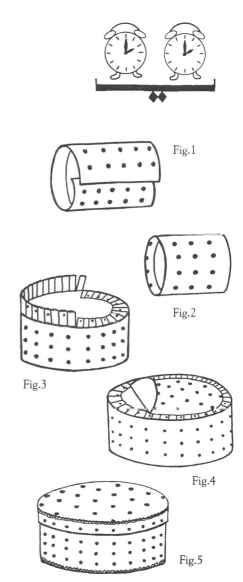

Fig.1

Fig.2

Fig.3

Fig.4

Fig.5

Flat-Folding Fabric or Paper-Covered Boxes

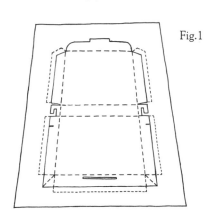

Fig.1

Cake, pie, and pizza boxes are the easiest to cover because they come in one flat piece and fold up into a box with a flap-type lid. Use a large enough piece of fabric or paper to cover the box. Spray mount adhesive on fabric or paste wallpaper on the wrong side. Place the box right side against glue. Line up design if using stripes or plaids. Flip box over and smooth any creases. Turn over again and trim around box, allowing 3/4-inch flaps for straight sides (Fig. 1). Glue down flaps to inside of box. Cut through notches in tabs (Fig. 2). Fold up into a box, slipping tabs into notches (Fig. 3).

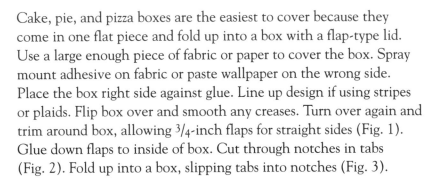

Fig.3

Fig.2

Bags

Bags are the simplest gift wrap of all. Even plain brown grocery bags or lunch sacks can be decorated with stickers, drawings, or any of the methods described in custom-printed papers. Large toys and oversized objects can be wrapped in a trash bag. With the proper paint job and the right ribbon no one will know where it came from. Need a fabric bag? How about using a pillowcase?

Ribbons and Bows

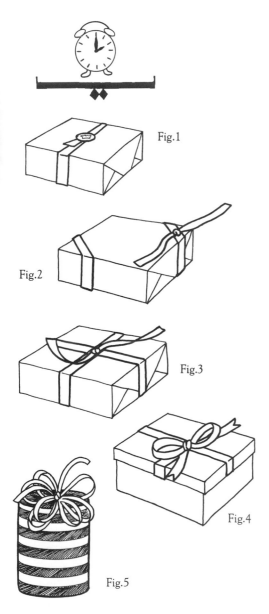

Fig.1

Fig.2

Fig.3

Fig.4

Fig.5

The right ribbon or bow is the crowning glory on a gift. From cascades of curling ribbon to crisp grosgrain and smooth satin, there are many types to choose from. Wired ribbon is in vogue, although it's been around for ages. Unconventional ties include lace, upholstery braid, raffia, rope, and even a necktie.

If cost is a factor, don't immediately go for cheap paper ribbon. Except to make a shredded chrysanthemum bow or a simple tailored band, it has little aesthetic value and is difficult to handle. Instead, opt for familiar curling ribbon. Both the old-fashioned type and the new metallics are extremely versatile. Colors can be blended and big wads of curls can be bound together for spectacular bows. Fine fabric ribbons are often found on sale throughout the year. Check out the bulk bins in fabric stores for some excellent buys and stock up while it's cheap. When using cloth ribbons, remember to treat the edges with a drop of fray-check solution to prevent unraveling.

Bows can be made from the wrap. For example, strips of Mylar tissue can be cut from the edge of a sheet. When the Mylar tissue is wrapped around a package, it's tied with the strips for a monochromatic effect. Folded paper fans or pinked tissue-paper pom-poms are other box-top embellishments.

When a bow is superfluous to the look of a package, a simple band of ribbon and a seal is all that's necessary to give a tailored presentation. An embossed, gold notary seal, or stamp of sealing wax is striking (Fig. 1).

Usually boxes are bound with ribbon, to which a bow is attached. The two most popular methods are: catching opposite corners (Fig. 2) or the crisscross (Fig. 3). When using the Hollywood Wrap technique, anchor edges of ribbon underneath the box lid, so that the package can be opened effortlessly (Fig. 4). There are times when the bow stands alone, particularly on round boxes (Fig. 5).

Shortcut-Chrysanthemum Bow

Decide upon the total diameter of your bow, then gather folds of ribbon, accordion style, in a stack of at least 8 folds (Fig. 1). Bind the stack in the center with a small piece of floral wire (Fig. 2). Fan out loops with your fingers to make a fluffy bow (Fig. 3).

Cropped-Chrysanthemum Bow

Follow the directions for making a traditional chrysanthemum bow. Then cut each loop in two, dividing ribbon into separate tails. Cut tails at angles (Fig. 4).

Split-Chrysanthemum Bow

Cut through loop edges of a traditional chrysanthemum bow (using paper ribbon only), dividing ribbon into separate tails. Using scissors and fingers, split tails of ribbon into several sections for an overall fringed effect (Fig. 5).

Curling-Ribbon Spray

The simplest way to make a splash with curling ribbon is to tie packages with multiple strands held together. This is very effective when the wrap is tied in a tassel. Leave streamers 8 to 12 inches long, and curl ends with scissors. (Fig. 6).

Curling Ribbon Pom-Pom Bow

This is a fun bow to make. I once made a huge bow the size of the box, consisting of 12 different colors.

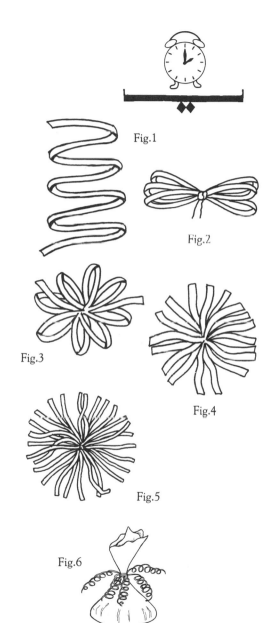

Fig.1

Fig.2

Fig.3

Fig.4

Fig.5

Fig.6

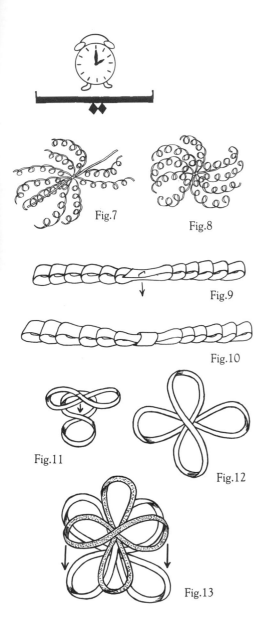

Fig.7

Fig.8

Fig.9

Fig.10

Fig.11

Fig.12

Fig.13

Large or small, multicolor or monochrome, the principle is the same: curl from one to twelve yards of ribbon with scissors. This doesn't have to be done in one continuous strand. You can curl several sections. Gather all the curled ribbon into one big, loose wad. Tie another piece of curling ribbon through the middle in a tight knot (Fig. 7). Curl streamers on the cross tie, then fluff up bow with your fingers (Fig. 8).

Tailored-Loop Bow

This bow can be made with inexpensive paper ribbon. It also looks very sophisticated when made with 1-inch wide grosgrain ribbon. Loop ribbon, back and forth in a graduated stack, the longest loop at the bottom. The stack should be from 3 to 5 loops deep, with each layer $1/2$ to 1 inch shorter on each end. Staple through all thicknesses in the center (Fig. 9). Cut a small piece of ribbon about $2^1/2$ inches long. Wrap around center of bow, concealing staple and securing at the bottom of the bow (Fig. 10). When assembling bow and anchoring ribbon on box, use double-stick tape for paper ribbon or a hot glue gun for fabric ribbon.

Figure-Eight Bow

Using self-sticking paper ribbon, this bow can grow as big as your box, in as many layers as you feel like making. Each layer is made with two figure eight shaped loops. Lengths of ribbon should be cut twice as long for the next layer.

Here's how to make a simple two-layer bow: cut 2 pieces of 9-inch-long ribbon and 2 pieces of 18-inch-long ribbon. Make figure eights out of loops, moistening edges to glue in place (Fig. 11). Attach same sized loops together, crossing in the centers, to form pinwheels (Fig. 12). Center smaller pinwheel over larger pinwheel so that

232

loops are at right angles to each other (Fig. 13). Glue in place. Cut a 3-inch strip of ribbon. Glue edges together into a small loop and glue into the center of the bow (Fig. 14).

Wired Bows

Commonly seen on wreaths, wired ribbon is so elegant that bows should be kept simple. Flexible wire in the selvages give bows life and wider ribbon is exceptionally striking. Always allow for long streamers that can be bent back and forth.

Simply take the length of ribbon and pinch loops on either side (Fig. 15). Cross ribbon over and tie in a basic bow (Fig. 16). Pull loops through so the center knot is somewhat full and not pinched looking (Fig. 17). With fingers shape loops and streamers (Fig. 18).

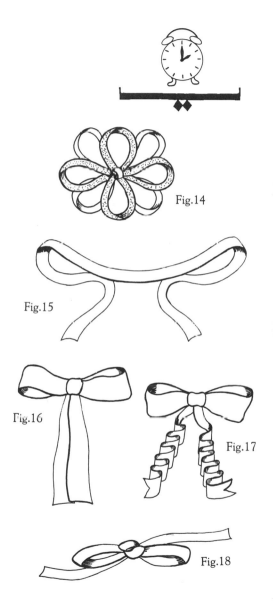

Fig.14

Fig.15

Fig.16

Fig.17

Fig.18

Box Toppers

There are many decorations that can be tied on top of a box. Silk or dried flowers, feathers, pinecones, bells, unusual buttons, even small toys are a few examples of box toppers. Rattles or bootees are often on top of baby gifts. A box topper can relate to the gift inside; for example, a wire whisk tied into the bow on a cookbook. Here are three bow alternatives you can make.

Silk or Dried-Flower Nosegay

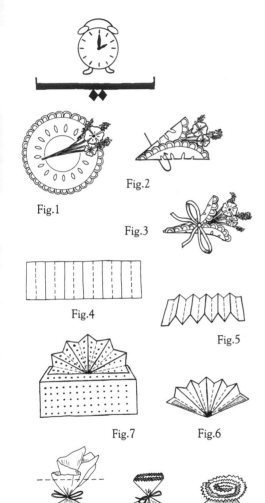

Fig.1

Fig.2

Fig.3

Fig.4

Fig.5

Fig.7

Fig.6

Fig.8

Fig.9

Fig.10

Place a small grouping of silk or dried flowers on a round cloth or paper doily (Fig. 1). The stems should be no longer than the doily, but flowers should peek out of the end when rolled up on a cone (Fig. 2). Tie a silk-ribbon bow around the middle of the cone (Fig. 3).

Paper Fans

Cut a strip of crisp wrapping paper about 20 inches long and 8 inches wide. Use a ruler to make neat 1-inch accordion-type folds, pressing creases with the ruler's edge (Fig. 4). Pinch fan together at base (Fig. 5). Connect along the bottom with a piece of tape (Fig. 6). Fan can be attached to the top of a box with double-stick tape (Fig. 7), so it is flat or stands straight up.

Tissue-Paper Pom-Poms

A common way of wrapping gifts in tissue paper is to surround it with layers of paper and gather it in a tassel at the top (Fig. 8). When different colors of paper have been used for several layers, this pom-pom effect can be quite dramatic. Cut through all layers of the tassel with pinking shears (Fig. 9). Spread out layers of tissue into a fluffy, carnation-like pom-pom (Fig. 10).

◆◆◆

CONVERSION TABLES

Outside the U.S., cooks measure more items by weight.
Here are approximate equivalents for basic items in this book.

	U.S. CUSTOMARY	METRIC	IMPERIAL
Apples (peeled and chopped)	2 cups	225 g	8 ounces
Butter	1 cup	225 g	8 ounces
	$1/2$ cup	115 g	4 ounces
	$1/4$ cup	60 g	2 ounces
	1 tablespoon	15 g	$1/2$ ounce
Chocolate chips	$1/2$ cup	85 g	3 ounces
Coconut (shredded)	$1/2$ cup	60 g	2 ounces
Flour (all purpose)	1 cup	150 g	5 ounces
Fruit (chopped)	1 cup	225 g	8 ounces
Nut Meats (chopped)	1 cup	115 g	4 ounces
Raisins (and other dried fruits)	1 cup	175 g	6 ounces
Sugar (granulated) or	1 cup	190 g	$61/2$ ounces
	$1/2$ cup	85 g	3 ounces
	$1/4$ cup	40 g	$13/4$ ounces
caster (confectioners')	1 cup	80 g	$22/3$ ounces
or icing	$1/2$ cup	40 g	$11/3$ ounces
	$1/4$ cup	20 g	$3/4$ ounce
brown	1 cup	160 g	$51/3$ ounces

OVEN TEMPERATURES					
Fahrenheit	225	300	350	400	450
Celsius	110	150	180	200	230
Gas Mark	$1/4$	2	4	6	8

235

LIQUID MEASURES

The Imperial pint is larger than the U.S. pint; therefore, note the following when measuring liquid ingredients.

U.S.	Imperial
1 cup = 8 fluid ounces	1 cup = 10 fluid ounces
1/2 cup = 4 fluid ounces	1/2 cup = 5 fluid ounces
1 tablespoon = 3/4 fluid ounce	1 tablespoon = 1 fluid ounce

U.S. Measure	Metric Approximate	Imperial Approximate
1 quart (4 cups)	950 mL	1 1/2 pints + 4 Tbsp
1 pint (2 cups)	450 mL	3/4 pint
1 cup	236 mL	1/4 pint + 6 Tbsp
1 Tbsp.	15 mL	1 + Tbsp
1 tsp.	5 mL	1 tsp

CONVERSION FROM ENGLISH TO METRIC

1 in.	=	25.4 mm
1 in.	=	2.54 cm
1 ft.	=	0.3 m
1 yd.	=	0.91 m
1 oz. (weight)	=	28.3 g
1 lb.	=	0.45 kg

CONVERSION FROM METRIC TO ENGLISH

1 mm	=	0.039 in.
1 cm	=	0.39 in.
1 m	=	3.28 ft.
1 m	=	1.09 yd.
1 g	=	0.04 oz.
1 kg	=	2.2 lb.

INDEX